EGO, AUTHORITY, FAILURE

EGO, AUTHORITY, FAILURE

USING EMOTIONAL INTELLIGENCE LIKE A HOSTAGE NEGOTIATOR TO SUCCEED AS A LEADER

DEREK GAUNT

Ego, Authority, Failure: Using Emotional Intelligence like a Hostage Negotiator to Succeed as a Leader

Hardcover ISBN: 978-1-5445-2686-7
Paperback ISBN: 978-1-5445-2684-3
eBook ISBN: 978-1-5445-2685-0

One of the deepest principles about life and leadership:
it's not about you.
–Ken Blanchard

This book is dedicated to all the people who have the courage to make themselves better and to all toxic leaders. Read and heed. You are doing more damage than you know.

CONTENTS

FOREWORD

By Christopher Voss, Founder and CEO of the Black Swan Group

IN THE VERY EARLY DAYS OF OUR NEGOTIATION CONSULTING company, the Black Swan Group, we were teaching a block of negotiation instruction within a leadership course being held in Germany. The attendees were members of the China Development Bank.

For an upcoming course that was only a couple of weeks away, I had a conflict, so I advised our German host that I had a substitute, Derek Gaunt, who was more qualified than me and a great lecturer. Andreas, our host, said, "Fine. I am sure if you recommend him, he is excellent."

Up to that point I had been one of Andreas's highest-rated instructors. He had been very pleased with my contribution and trusted me.

"How many times has he taught this course?" Andreas asked.

My reply? "Never."

"Never?" Andreas's voice shot up about two octaves. He sounded like a teenage boy whose voice was just beginning to change.

Andreas was in a bind. We were just too close to the course date for him to conduct an entirely new search for someone else.

"Can I at least talk to him first?" Andreas pleaded.

"Sure," I said, and we set it up.

The conversation between Andreas and Derek went well enough that it adequately soothed Andreas's fears, and Derek went out and taught the course.

The next time Andreas called me for his course, he said, "Hey, you are busy again, right? You have got to send Derek again, right?"

I was one of Andreas's highest-rated instructors—until Derek became *the* highest-rated instructor ever. Andreas told me that on a five-point scale, Derek was the only one ever rated a straight five. And the members of the China Development Bank were the toughest raters he had had.

To make things even worse (for my ego), Derek and I were later discussing the training, and he said, "Man, going to that graduation dinner is tough! Those guys drink and toast like nobody I ever saw, and they expect you to keep up with them! How did you handle it?"

I said, "I did not. They never invited me to the dinner."

Derek Gaunt knows about leadership. Derek Gaunt knows about hostage negotiations. He teaches them both exceptionally. In *Ego, Authority, Failure* he marries both disciplines to provide cautionary tales and actionable skills to improve leadership performance.

I wrote about Derek in the acknowledgments section of my book *Never Split the Difference: Negotiating as If Your Life Depended on It*. Derek has been a great wingman and a great friend since I first arrived in the Washington, DC, area two decades ago.

Derek became one of the most important hostage negotiators in the Washington metropolitan area. And that includes local, state, and federal agencies.

He founded or co-founded two different regional hostage negotiation associations that everyone in the DC metro area who wanted to get better at their job attended. Everyone knew him, and when important issues came up that affected the profession, everyone wanted to know what Derek thought.

He personally organized multiagency exercises that hostage negotiators from state, local, and federal agencies attended. He organized weeklong training courses that everyone attended. Even SWAT guys and the regional SWAT association supported Derek.

The hostage negotiators on his team at the Alexandria (Virginia) Police Department (and later the Alexandria Sheriff's Office) were top notch and knew it was because of Derek's leadership and dedication to both them and their craft.

Across the board, he is that good. It is my privilege to know him.

Read this book.

INTRODUCTION

I BEGAN MY LAW ENFORCEMENT CAREER IN 1988. AFTER TWO years as a patrol officer, I was selected to join an elite, plain-clothes, street-level narcotics unit. My job was to enforce narcotics violations and the accompanying nuisance-related crimes. At the time we were known as the "jump-out" based on the way we conducted our enforcement.

Seemingly out of nowhere, we would arrive on the scene of a street-level narcotics transaction, jump out of our rental cars, and effect the arrest. Then we would just as quickly leave the scene. To a bystander, it looked like a kidnapping. In fact, many bystanders called 911 to report just that when we were making an arrest.

After the arrest, the dealers and buyers would often look for a way out of their charges by cooperating with us, provid-ing information on other dealers or buyers. Sometimes they provided information on more serious crimes.

In these instances, I began to hone my interview and interrogation skills.

I learned if I could say the right thing in the right way, I could elicit a specific response. I was hooked. I wanted to learn more. I attended a Wicklander-Zulawski interrogation class. I was also trained in the Reid Technique of Interrogation and was especially interested in the psychology behind using empathy to uncover information without the bad guy knowing what I was doing. It was a rush. I knew I wanted more. I wanted to be a detective.

In 1994 I got my chance.

When I was a detective, a significant part of my job was to try to get information from people who fell into one of three categories:

1. They did not want to provide information that would expose them any further to the criminal justice system.

2. They were traumatized by the event.

3. They were afraid of the repercussions if someone found out they had given information to the police.

Each of the categories required rapport building to allay their concerns and gain their trust so they would willingly provide the information. Building rapport and gathering information was the way to go. I learned this long before the post-9/11 studies on detainee interrogation, one of which stated, "Detainees were fourteen times more likely to disclose information earlier in an interview when the interviewer used rapport-building strategies."

After a few years of this, I wanted to take this passion to the next level as a hostage negotiator. Many of the negotiators on the team were detectives, which supported the idea that similar skillsets were found in both disciplines.

In 1997, I competed for and was selected to fill one of five spots on our Hostage Negotiation Team (HNT). Immediately I became a student of the game. I immersed myself in everything related to empathy, interpersonal communication, and hostage/barricade management. I was promoted through the ranks, becoming team supervisor in 2001 and then team commander in 2004, a position I held until my retirement in 2014.

I saw a lot, did a lot, and learned a lot about human nature, psychology, emotion, and communication. Over the years, I saw firsthand how important it is to calibrate communication to de-escalate emotional responses and turn negative situations into positives so people can return to, as the FBI's Crisis Negotiations Unit puts it, the NFL—the normal functioning level.

HOSTAGE NEGOTIATOR LEADERSHIP

As you will see in this book, that is what Hostage Negotiator Leadership (HNL) is all about.

When people learn what I do, I frequently get a series of Hollywood-inspired questions:

"Were you like Denzel Washington in *Inside Man*?"

"Have you shot anyone?"

"How many times was your life in danger?"

It is a common conversation for me, so instead of playing up the drama, I like to use my training to turn the attention away from me, prompting others to share more about *their* lives and work experiences.

Most people seem a bit embarrassed to talk about their work; they seem to think that what they do on a daily basis pales in comparison to what I do (or did). But with a little empathetic listening, I am nearly always able to get them to share more.

And here is the fascinating thing. The challenges at their jobs and with their bosses or employees nearly always remind me of my work with hostages and hostage-takers. Their stories contain all the common denominators in hostage negotiations: a negative emotional component, resistance, and difficult conversation. As I thought more about these experiences, it became clear to me that hostage negotiations are just difficult conversations.

When you look at the cover of this book, you might ask, "How can hostage negotiation skills be applied to leadership?"

All leaders, regardless of the environment, come in contact with the same psychological, emotional, and communications challenges that stem from human nature. Let us take sales, for example. Ultimately, sales is about compliance: you have to convince someone else that what you have to offer is better than what they have now. In Daniel Pink's 2012 book *To Sell Is Human,* he shows how even non-sales professionals spend up to 40 percent of their day trying to influence their peers or change their peers' behavior in one way or another.

As a hostage negotiator, I was the ultimate compliance professional. I sold jail time, and I got hostage-takers to buy what I was selling. An armed hostage-taker, with seemingly all the leverage, eventually agreed with me that spending the next twenty years behind bars was better than the alternative—not just because the twenty SWAT guys surrounding the crisis site were ready, willing, and able to rock his world but because I built enough rapport and trust-based influence with him.

David Nye, Chief of Police in Fredericksburg, Virginia, once said, "I have never been a negotiator, but it seems to me there are a lot of parallels between leadership and hostage negotiations. It is how you treat people. Do they feel like they matter? Do they feel like you care about them at all? In your negotiations, it is listening to him and showing some empathy. You matter. I care. Yeah, there are a lot of parallels to leadership."

What if you began to treat your employees with the same level of deference and thoughtfulness as negotiators do hostage-takers?

What if you showed your employees that you could subordinate yourself to them?

What if you began to realize and act as if it was not all about you?

I believe Hostage Negotiator Leadership will bring these questions to the front of your mind, increasing your ability to handle difficult conversations and helping you become a more effective leader.

The concept of EQ was introduced in 1990 by Peter Salovey and John D. Mayer and then taken on a deeper dive in 1995 by Daniel Goleman when he penned a book of the same name. In the intervening twenty-eight years, many more books have been written espousing the virtues of EQ in leadership. But here we are, still talking about the same problem: the perpetual lack of it.

Even in highly successful companies with leaders who may be perceived well, employees frequently cite their boss as the primary reason they leave their job. Common factors that contribute to employee departure are management style, condescending attitudes, and cruelty. This is what happens when ego and authority take over.

Makes sense, but why is this the case? Why are poor management style, condescension, and ill temper so prevalent?

There are several reasons.

First, some leaders fixate on maintaining or enhancing their self-image.

Second, ego is an emotion that clouds judgment, and authority supports and feeds ego.

Third, not enough leaders learn how to demonstrate empathy beyond a generic facade. Bosses are told, "Do not be a jerk," "Listen to your employees," "Build relationships," "Communicate better." All of these are touted as necessary for leadership success. But how do you do it?

I began to answer this question for myself by viewing my subordinates and colleagues with the same level of attention and consideration as I would in a hostage crisis. In the simplest terms, once you begin to treat every employee like a hostage-taker and every difficult conversation like a negotiation where you are the negotiator, you will think, act, and speak differently.

In the United States, hostage negotiators have a success rate of over 90 percent in influencing surrender.

What is your success rate of influencing others?

Even the most influential people are probably only

successful about 35–40 percent of the time. Why the disparity? Is it because hostage negotiators are smarter than everybody else? Hardly. It is because we are versed in skills that are based on the human-nature response.

Once you understand human nature and seriously consider what is important to the other person—what they value, their environment, or their circumstances—you can make more informed predictions about your outcomes and become a more successful leader.

The framework you will discover in *Ego, Authority, Failure* is designed to facilitate a change in the way leaders and managers think about communicating with peers, superiors, and direct reports. It will teach you the skills necessary to listen better, get more positive outcomes, create happier employees, and maintain a better workplace environment.

HOW TO READ THIS BOOK

In almost thirty years of law enforcement and hostage negotiations, I have been a part of many incidents involving life and death as well as hundreds of practical scenarios and training activities. In that time, I have helped hundreds of people apply the principles of hostage negotiations to everyday leadership.

In this book, you will hear stories at the intersection of hostage negotiation skills and leadership performance to demonstrate:

- What makes the good leaders good and the bad ones bad.

- How ego can negatively influence everything, including life-and-death decisions.

- The power and purpose of emotional intelligence and *Tactical Empathy.*

Like you, I have witnessed and been victimized by leaders whose ego and authority created what is commonly referred to as a toxic work environment. I saw or reported to the narcissist, the bully, the incompetent, the indecisive, and the liar. Most of these leaders were smart. They had the capacity to be better. But they were never taught the basic interpersonal skills necessary to demonstrate empathy or manage their ego and authority.

Throughout the book I will provide examples of leaders and organizations that illustrate how important developing these skills can be. I will use the terms *significant conversations* and *difficult conversations* interchangeably. Both refer to situations where the parties in the conversation need to stay in a relationship, the stakes are high, opinions vary, and negative emotions are bubbling just below the surface and could boil over.

In recent years I have interviewed leaders from the corporate, law enforcement, military, and sports worlds—all of whom, without realizing it, engaged some of the positive response tactics tested and proven in the discipline of hostage negotiations. These techniques helped them to connect or feel connected to those within their environments. You can think of these examples as case studies to show how applicable and effective these principles are.

The ultimate goal of *Ego, Authority, Failure* is application. If you apply these skills, you will perform at a higher level. Whether you are a C-suite executive, midlevel manager, athletic coach, front-line supervisor, or human relations professional, this book was written for you. Each of you has some authority over or responsibility for someone else within your organization. Keeping the skills in this book at the top of your mind will vastly improve your interactions with them.

To get the most out of the book, use Parts I and II to acquaint yourself with key components of the HNL framework, along with the successes and failures of other leaders. Throughout the book I will share some case studies, allowing the stories to speak for themselves. These leaders' and their organizations' statuses are not as important as the lessons we all can learn from them. These are ordinary bosses who did the best and worst they could within their environments. Part III is focused on moving from understanding to action. The goal is for you to build the skills you need to improve your outcomes in significant conversations in the following ways:

- Improving your leadership performance by becoming a proactive, strategic, and intuitive listener.

- Establishing, maintaining, or repairing damaged superior–subordinate relationships.

- Managing your ego and authority.

- Navigating difficult conversations, change, and dissension.

- Increasing your proficiency in gathering information and influencing others.

These techniques were perfected by cops for cops. They are simple, readily available for recall, and effective because that is what cops want more than anything else. These techniques are designed to create what we call *trust-based influence* in order to motivate and inspire people to achieve unexpected, even extraordinary, results.

The principles and stories in this book are drawn from my own experiences and those of mid- to executive-level leaders. Others have been culled from open sources. Some of the people interviewed are still employed at the organizations in which they experienced leadership abuse of ego and authority. With the exception of the open-sourced individuals, names have been changed to honor the anonymity of those interviewed as well as the less-admirable leaders I highlight. The goal for me is not to focus on the individuals as much as their behavior. It is a mirror reflecting how you are seen by many of your subordinates and others—as arrogant, self-serving, inflexible, and petty. The stories of the toxic leaders in the book are not unique to any one space. You will recognize all of them based on your own experiences.

This book is for leaders who are in denial about the damage their ego and authority have on their organization. It is also for people who have the courage to make themselves better.

PART I

THE CORE PRINCIPLES OF HOSTAGE NEGOTIATOR LEADERSHIP

CHAPTER 1

THE CRISIS OF LEADERSHIP AND THE HOSTAGE NEGOTIATOR FRAMEWORK

THE CRISIS: EGO AND AUTHORITY

WE HAVE ALL EXPERIENCED BAD LEADERSHIP. WHETHER WE have been the recipient or the one responsible, we know that misuse of authority produces pain and disappointment.

What research shows again and again is that ego and authority are the mother and father of toxic leadership. They instill fear. They influence the actions of coworkers and employees creating anger, resentment, mistrust, and hostility. When these characteristics become a part of an organization's culture, quality of life and retention rates plummet.

Abraham Lincoln once said, "If you want to discover just what there is in a man—give him power. It will either make him or wreck him."

The Hostage Negotiator Leadership (HNL) framework is designed to make us better, by understanding that ego and authority are not 100 percent evil. The lack of understanding and the absence of self-control are what wrecks us and those we lead. The highest-performing organizations have exceptional leaders who have figured out how to cultivate emotional intelligence (EQ) and what I call Tactical Empathy to get the best from their teams. This book explains how.

It also serves as a contrast to much of what has been said about EQ up to this point. If you search Google for the terms "business leaders and EQ," you will find a trove of articles, books, and blog posts, with new material emerging every day to advocate for the importance of EQ in leadership. But very few of them give you the skills necessary to improve your EQ or enhance your ability to demonstrate empathy.

The goal I want to work toward is for you to become a better leader by improving your interpersonal communications and EQ by using the HNL framework that relies on the following principles:

- Focusing on the process, not the objective. Navigate the conversation, zeroing in *what* is being said and *why* as opposed to focusing on the end result.

- Understanding the importance of sequencing. The proper sequencing is Tactical Empathy first, your objective last.

- Gathering information. Navigating tough conversations is an exercise in guided discovery where you actively seek new information about your counterpart.

- Demonstrating Tactical Empathy. Show your counterpart that you understand the way they view the circumstances.

- Understanding the human-nature response. Negative emotions and dynamics are significant drivers of human decision-making and behavior.

- Creating safe and inclusive environments. Establish a workplace environment free of unnecessary commentary where input is encouraged.

- Using tone, delivery, and projected sincerity. How you say it is much more important than what you say.

HNL has many moving parts, so it is critical for you to be cognizant of the various factors that impact your effectiveness in improving your relationships with colleagues and the people who work for you. First and foremost, it is hard work!

TOUGH CONVERSATIONS

No one really likes to engage in tough conversations. If you close your eyes right now and think about a real or imagined difficult conversation, it is probably not a pleasant thought. You will likely conjure up an image of a snarling, aggressive, crying, hysterical, or manipulative counterpart who tries to impose their will or otherwise paint you into a corner.

Tough conversations create stress. Stress constricts thinking and makes us uncomfortable. When we are uncomfortable, we want more than anything to be comfortable again—as quickly as possible. The sooner you solve the problem, the sooner the tough conversation will be over. The sooner the tough conversation is over, the sooner you can get out of the room. The sooner you can get out of the room, the sooner your comfort level returns. This "sequencing" causes leaders to compromise their position, violate rules, or deviate from best practices.

I like to drive this point home with a short negotiation exercise called *sixty seconds* that I often use with corporate training groups. I ask for three volunteers and move them outside the main room. Then I explain to the non-volunteers what is about to happen.

For the purpose of this exercise, I am a bank robber. I have no other gainful employment. When I want to put food on the table or clothes on my back or buy some of the finer things in life, I rob banks. And I am good—except today I got caught, and now I am trapped inside the bank.

The volunteers, who play the role of the hostage negotiator, do not know how many accomplices I have. They do not know how many hostages there are, and they are not permitted to negotiate about the following items:

- Drugs or alcohol

- Weapons and ammunition

- Transportation

- Exchange of hostages

These items are prohibited by almost every law enforcement agency in the country.

I then bring the volunteers back into the room and give them the ground rules. Once they have gotten themselves together, I have them "ring" the phone, and the exercise begins.

I answer and say, "I want a car in sixty seconds or she dies," in an aggressive tone. Most stammer a response, ask me my name, or deny the request and then immediately switch to bargaining with me (i.e., problem-solving).

Them: Uh...can I have your name?

Me: You do not need to know my name! You now have fifty seconds! (The stress created by my elevated voice and tone becomes apparent.)

Them: (Sigh) Shit. What kind of car do you want? What type of transportation do you need? (One of the four things that I explicitly told them they could not bring up. Stress.)

Me: I will let you make the determination on that. Two-door. Four-door. It does not matter to me. I just want you to pull it up out front, leave the keys in the ignition, and leave the driver's door open.

Them: How many people are gonna be in the car? I need to know.

Me: It is just gonna be me. I am coming out by myself.

Them: By yourself? (Great *Mirror*)

Me: By myself. How long is it gonna take? You have got forty seconds!

Them: Where are you going?

Me: I am not gonna divulge where I am going. Just know that I am leaving here. You have thirty seconds!

Them: Is there anything else you need?

Me: I did not ask for anything else! I asked you for a car! You have got twenty-five seconds!

Them: Okay. We are working on it.

Me: All right. Let's do it. What are you gonna do? You gonna call me back?

Them: Well, I am gonna see if I can find you a car.

Me: Are you serious? There are fifty of you out there. I am confident that one of you dummies drove here today! Get me that car!

Them: (Under their breath) I think I had better find a car. (To me) Okay. We are working on it. We are gonna pull it up right out front, and you are gonna come out the front door? What else do you need? What else do you need to feel comfortable...to end this situation? You are just gonna—you are just gonna drive the car away? All by yourself?

Me: You let me know when it is my time to talk.

Them: What is that?

Me: You let me know when it is my turn to talk. You are dominating the conversation.

Them: I am just asking you what you need to make you feel comfortable. I—

Me: Can I talk?

Them: Sure. Absolutely.

Me: I do not need anything else. I did not ask you for anything else. I just want the car. You said you were gonna pull it up out front. I just need to know how long it is gonna take because I need to get ready.

Them: We can do it in a few minutes.

Me: A few minutes? Great. Just let me know when it is there, and I will walk out. You have my word.

Them: Okay. We have the car identified.

Me: Okay.

Them: Uh...it is coming around front. There is gonna be a police officer there. He is gonna leave the keys in the ignition and leave the door open.

The exercise clearly demonstrates that stress and pressure, born out of the emotion of fear, cause the participants to compromise, jump prematurely into problem-solving, and break rules, all so they can get comfortable again. The same dynamics occur in difficult conversations every day.

As a leader, it is common to go into tough conversations driving for a yes with employees, peers, or supervisors. But HNL does not prioritize your *yes*. That comes later.

Instead, HNL prioritizes the *why*. What are the underlying motivations and emotions that are driving the behavior of the other person? This requires the use of Tactical Empathy, which is the deliberate attempt to recognize and articulate another's perspective.

Once you understand Tactical Empathy, at the deepest level, then you are in a position to:

- Resolve the issue.

- Make your ask.

- State your objective.

- Satisfy the needs of the other person.

Bottom line? It is not about you. It is about them. And it is about discovering their why without asking why.

SELF-CONTROL

To engage others in significant conversations where emotions run high, keeping your wits about you is crucial to a positive outcome. When confronted with these situations, the first thing to do is control your own emotions and behavior rather than trying to control the emotions and behavior of the other person. If you cannot control yourself, you cannot effectively direct the discussion. If you respond to an attack or to anger with anger, you become part of the problem, not the solution.

Do not confuse getting even with getting what you want. If the conversation is confrontational, work toward de-escalation.

Do not punish with words. Focus on the process of satisfying the other person's needs rather than working toward a predetermined outcome.

A calm, controlled demeanor is usually more effective than a brilliant argument.

UNDERSTANDING PEOPLE, BUILDING RELATIONSHIPS

To understand people, you have to build and maintain relationships. Leaders often possess four attitudes, which interfere with building and maintaining relationships:

- Black-and-white thinking

- A belief that feelings are not important

- Ability to quickly solve problems

- Inflexibility

Black-and-white thinking plays into our tendency to look for what is easy to comprehend. Cognitive overload is a pain in the head. At the same time, leaders like to think of themselves as smart. Intellectually, we understand that the world is complex, but we still find ourselves drawn into viewing things as either black or white in an increasingly gray world. Good or evil. Right or wrong. Yes or no.

Black-and-white thinking is not fundamentally bad until

it generates a false dichotomy that clouds our vision and judgment. As the adage goes, there are two sides to every story, and then there is the truth.

Feelings are important, which is critical for successful leaders to understand. Like it or not, people make decisions based on how they feel, no matter how left-brained they might be. It is impossible to remove emotions from the decision-making process, so telling employees to ignore theirs or others' happens at your organization's peril. Focus your attention on motivation and driving forces to build collaborative teams. Yes, your people need you to have operational awareness, but they also need you to have good interpersonal skills and emotional awareness.

If you can combine rational skills with EQ, you can transform who you are as a leader and increase the satisfaction of the people who work around you.

Quick problem-solving is definitely a useful skill. But sometimes when someone approaches you with a problem, they do not just want your help in solving it. Sometimes they just want you to listen.

As a leader, you are expected to adhere to the organization's mission and help it grow, which requires a lot of problem-solving. Too often, though, we rush to a particular outcome at the expense of understanding. Think about it. How often does your company actually encourage people to slow down and think? Most do not. How much problem-solving could be accomplished simply by listening to the personnel?

Whether navigating a difficult conversation or making critical decisions, showing restraint and being patient offers the best results. Rushing toward the outcome without listening, focusing on the process, or identifying the why is a recipe for failure.

Inflexibility happens when we come up with a plan of action and refuse to budge. But rigidity is a pacifier for weak or insecure leaders. Inflexible leaders push forward when it would be smarter to adapt or consider the input of others. Rigid leaders relish command and control. It is "my way or the highway." These leaders confuse compliance with bona fide team ownership or buy-in. As a result, they reject input from highly talented employees because they perceive these employees as threats. Perhaps most damaging of all, rigid leaders do not listen.

Flexible leaders utilize multiple approaches and have the ability to adjust to each team member or situation. They modify their style in accordance with uncertain or unpredictable circumstances and recognize situations in which they do not know it all. Strive to be flexible and creative in your approach to leading your team.

Do not say never. Say, "It depends."

LISTEN

As I pointed out above, listening is the easiest and most affordable way to find common ground and create a positive atmosphere for problem-solving at the appropriate time. Do not argue. Give people a "hearing," and allow them to vent. People want to be understood. Listen to them. Acknowledge their points. Acknowledgment does not equate to agreement. Agree whenever you can—without conceding.

Also bear in mind that most people do not always say what they mean. They ask the wrong questions or couch messages within statements. Good listening will help you go beneath the surface to understand what the other person is really trying to say. Your challenge is to listen for underlying emotion or meaning. Part of your responsibility as a leader is to balance the sometimes-extensive list of "demands" made by your employees with the needs of the organization as you come to a resolution or agreement.

It is going to take some work.

Much of the work will be getting your head around the five different levels of listening.

1. **Intermittent listening** is listening long enough to get the gist before refocusing on your internal voice, reactions, and thoughts. This is your frame of reference.

2. **Listening for rebuttals** is listening to their point of view long enough so you can rebut it or until you hear something that triggers a reaction that you can argue with. Then you are just waiting for them to stop talking so you can interject.

3. **Listening for the internal logic** of what they are saying, using a lot of inference, is next. If this is their world-view, conclusion, or judgment—the story they are telling—what is their data? What is the reasoning or

interpretation? What is the rationale behind what they are saying? Why does it make sense to them?

4. **Listening for the emotions and identity issues** attached to the argument is the next level. What frustrations, anxiety, despair, or betrayal are driving the argument? They may or may not line up logically for you, but they are certainly a part of what the person is trying to express as they talk about what is important to them.

5. **Listening for their life's narrative** is the deepest level. How does this match who they are in the world? What meaning do they give it? How do they view the lay of the land? What are their circumstances? What does their message symbolize or represent?

We put that filter of recognition on top of emotion and logic. This goes beyond, "Oh yeah, I get where they are coming from" to deeply appreciating their environment and motivations.

If you do not understand their worldview, you do not understand them. If you do not understand them, you cannot influence them. Listening at level five takes effort and energy— too much to operate at it 24/7. Most of us operate at levels two and three most of the day. Your challenge as a leader is to be able to engage at the fifth level when it counts.

TAKEAWAYS

- Difficult conversations make people uncomfortable, stressed, and prone to bad decision-making.

- Maintaining self-control involves understanding your triggers in the face of pressure or an attack.

- Inflexible leaders build resistance to considering alternatives.

- Revenge is not a strategy.

- Listening, connecting, and empathizing puts you in a better position to take appropriate action.

CHAPTER 2

PEOPLE FIRST

HOSTAGE NEGOTIATOR LEADERSHIP (HNL) REQUIRES A people-first approach and asks us to subordinate ourselves to the person we are in conversation with. This might not fit in with most of what we have heard about leadership or with many organizations that think they have it all figured out. But it is an approach that will open leaders to a life of learning committed to authenticity, transparency, and empathy.

Theories of leadership abound, from business schools to corporate training organizations. But business schools do not spend nearly enough time preaching (teaching) the virtues of empathy, so their graduates enter the workforce with self-serving attitudes. Similarly, many CEOs say empathy is important, but data shows there is a lack of interpersonal communication skills training within organizations. This coupled with what is going on in business schools creates fertile ground for toxic leadership.

Nelson Mandela once said, "A leader is like a shepherd. He stays behind the flock, letting the most nimble go out ahead, whereupon the others follow, not realizing that all along they are being directed from behind." The HNL model takes this wisdom, creating an environment where you ultimately improve the lives of your employees and keep them engaged and committed to the mission.

I have seen firsthand how the HNL's people-first mindset can play out.

SUBORDINATING YOURSELF

Here is a real-life example of what can happen when we put others first.

The Cash Store pawnshop was located in a strip mall we affectionately dubbed "Hostage Row," having been the scene of previous hostage-takings. It sat on King Street in Alexandria, Virginia, on the border with Arlington County.

The hostage-taker's name was Mike. Mike enlisted the help of a buddy, Steve, to rob the pawnshop. They drove to the strip mall and parked a few spots down from the front of the business. Both exited the car and donned ski masks. Mike produced a handgun as they entered the business and announced the robbery to the five customers and three employees.

Their day went downhill from there.

When they entered the pawnshop, a twelve-year-old boy was riding his bike to the Five Guys hamburger joint located in Hostage Row just around the corner from the pawnshop. He reported what he saw to the manager of the Five Guys, who called the police. Two units were parked nearby and responded in less than ninety seconds.

The units approached the rear of the business with weapons drawn. Using a trash compactor for cover, one officer,

Jeff, pointed his shotgun at the rear of the business. The other, Adrienne, was at a ninety-degree angle on Jeff's left, pointing her service weapon at the door. As Jeff got on the radio to coordinate the other officers' response, the back door of the pawnshop flew open, and there stood Mike and Steve. Jeff was surprised to see them. They were surprised to see him. Jeff challenged Mike and Steve: "Police! Don't move!" Mike responded by slamming the door shut.

The hostage-taking was on.

Dana, the founder of our hostage negotiation team (HNT), built our team out of nothing and made it into one of the preeminent HNTs in the Washington metropolitan area. He had reached the stage in his career where he was teaching more than negotiating, but on this day he found himself as the primary negotiator in a very dangerous incident.

It had been almost ten years since we had had a hostage-taking of this scope, and in that one, we lost two officers.

Nerves were on edge.

Dana called the pawnshop's phone. When Mike eventually picked up, Dana embodied the HNL model, immediately deferring in conversation.

"Hey. My name is Dana, I—"

"Look, man, do not come in here. If you all do anything foolish, these people gonna get hurt, man! Blood is gonna be on your hands."

"Nobody is coming in there. Okay? You have my word on that. We just wanna make sure you are okay. What happened? How did we get here today?"

From the very start, Dana conveyed to Mike that this event was about him. Not the hostages. Not the police. Of course, Dana's ultimate goal was to get Mike to release the hostages and surrender, but he did not mention or focus on that during the initial dialogue. It was all about demonstrating for Mike that we understood his worldview even if we were not in agreement with his current actions.

By subordinating himself to Mike, Dana showed more concern for Mike than anything else. The result? Mike admitted that his name was not Mike. It was Keith. Dana returned Keith to a (more) normal functioning level where he began to see the hostages had nothing to do with his current circumstances. After an hour he released the first group. Shortly thereafter he released the remaining hostages before killing himself.

Dana earned trust that was key to achieving the release of the hostages. It is counterintuitive for most people to ignore their objectives during difficult conversations, but Dana knew the power in these subtle overtures. With two questions, he put Keith first, and that move would pay big dividends before the end of the incident.

Putting your people before yourself will likewise pay big dividends in your role as a leader.

HUMILITY AND SINCERITY

Retired United States Army Colonel William Montgomery III is a senior lead technologist for a major defense contracting firm. In 2007, he wrote a strategy research project paper entitled, "Beyond Words: Leader Self-Awareness and Interpersonal Skills."

As a major in 2001, Montgomery worked for a battalion commander who told him that effective leadership went beyond the army doctrine of "listen to your leaders, do not ask a lot of questions, move out, and get the mission done." He told Montgomery effective leadership was about taking care of your people.

Both Montgomery and the battalion commander agreed that the Army was not doing the best it could when it came to connecting with people. Montgomery was encouraged to attend a leadership training course at Fort Leavenworth, Kansas. The battalion commander said the course would shake him up a bit and be invigorating before Montgomery became a battalion commander.

When Montgomery approached his direct supervisor about attending the course, he did not receive an immediate favorable response. "Why are you going to Leavenworth to learn what you have been learning in the military for the last eighteen years? You already know leadership. Why do you want to be a part of a civilian course when you have had these deployment experiences?" Montgomery explained his reasons, and his supervisor granted permission for him to attend.

The fourteen days he spent at Fort Leavenworth allowed him to compare and contrast current civilian leadership training with that of the army. There were twenty-five people in the class, all civilians except for Montgomery. The course was mandated for army civilian employees if they wanted to get promoted to a GS-14 or higher. The facilitators worked with them through what he called "the experience," which allowed them to self-assess and take stock of their ability to interact with individuals they had never met before.

The class was together twelve to fourteen hours a day, including weekends. It took this group of total strangers through the four stages of team development, and at times the road of "the experience" was quite bumpy.

Montgomery reported instances where the conflict bubbled to the surface and fights nearly broke out. More than once he questioned his rationale for being there.

This was actually a part of the plan. The facilitators explained that allowing conflict to play out in the learning environment was a necessity. They would see this type of conflict in the real world, so it was something the facilitators were not willing to stifle.

After the course, Montgomery was indeed invigorated, and he took with him leadership lessons of "the experience" as he continued on his way to becoming a battalion commander.

To bolster the training received at Leavenworth, the facilitators offered to conduct mini-workshops for the class participants once they returned to their regular duty stations. Montgomery took them up and invited one of them to Japan to deliver a three-day workshop to a group of people he had never met: his new battalion.

The workshop was structured in a way that it took all the noncommissioned officers (NCOs) and civilian leadership away from the battalion for three full days. There were murmurings about how the training would adversely impact them, with so much of the leadership missing for three days. Many said

Montgomery was foolish for making the attempt and would not likely recover if the training indeed disrupted operations.

"It is interesting," Montgomery said, "that 90 percent of the folks I talked to, who were my peers, who were also going into this experience, immediately told me, 'Bill, do not do this. You do not need to.'"

Fortunately, the facilitator he met at Leavenworth was encouraging. He said, "Look, Bill, this is exactly what you are going to hear. This is exactly what you heard as you rose through the ranks. So you have got two choices. You can either go with your gut because you have experienced this and trust that this will do more for your group, or you can forget about it and chalk it up as a great experience for yourself. Unfortunately, if you do that, you are not really going to be able to empower the folks you are actually there to lead, and you are not gonna gain anything."

Another piece of advice the facilitator gave to Montgomery was to take his newly discovered trusting and transparent leadership style and apply it with vigor during his first seventy-two hours on the base.

"If you do," the facilitator said, "you will learn things about the organization, yourself, and the leaders you have now taken under your wing."

Unfortunately, most leaders do not take the time to learn about the people within their organizations until they are six or seven months in. By then, it is usually too late because they have become so mired in the obstacles, tasks, and requirements of their new position that they do not have the time to discern what is *really* going on with their personnel.

Two weeks prior to his new assignment in Japan, Montgomery was still undecided as to whether to execute the three-day training. He was afraid he was going to blow it. However, he knew the value of the program. He knew leaders do not get many opportunities at experiences like this. Intuition told him to go with the training, but his head was telling him he was a new battalion commander in a foreign country. *You are taking a huge risk, dummy.* He wrestled with the decision for a few days but ultimately went with his gut.

Montgomery changed command on a Friday. The facilitators went to work the same day, conducting interviews through the weekend. They interviewed all the senior leadership, asking thought-provoking questions: "How are things going?" "What are some things you would like to see change?" "How do you feel?"

The first session started at eight o'clock Monday morning and continued through Wednesday. The facilitator told him he needed to display sincerity and authenticity, adding, "Leaders go first. Good leaders are transparent, and that is the way you have got to go into this group. You need to be very authentic. The first hour you are with them, you want the rest of the group to believe that what they are seeing is real. It is not some kind of an experiment." He sat down with the group, subordinated himself, and then shared the story of his two weeks in Leavenworth.

The civilians in attendance had served under five or six different commanders. What they were being exposed to as the training got underway was in stark contrast to what they were accustomed to, but they gave it a chance because of

Montgomery's humility and sincerity. He told them, "I really believe this will do great things for you. Not only as a unit but in your marriage, social life, community, whatever. It is going to stay with you."

Initially, everybody looked around at each other, confused, as if to ask what they were doing there.

Eventually, there came a revelation, and by close of business Wednesday, Montgomery knew he had hit the mark.

His most vivid memory was of a command sergeant major who was an E-9 with twenty-seven years in the military. He broke down in tears at the end of the final group session where they were sitting in a circle and reflecting on the three-day journey they had undertaken. The reasons for the E-9's tears were both joy and relief. He said he was unaware of the way the team viewed his wife.

Montgomery said, "Wives play a big part in organizations, and apparently the sergeant major's wife was so involved in the organization that she kind of wore the rank of her husband, and that was a barrier for many of the soldiers."

The E-9 basically said, "I am so thankful that we took this approach because I learned things about myself as well as my wife and, more importantly, how to help the group in ways I never would have. There is still time to turn it into a positive when it comes to listening and being more authentic as opposed to just thinking everything is going fine."

As good as the workshop was, Montgomery's job was not done. The facilitator told him that if he wanted this organizational leadership experience to stick, he should allow them to come back in six and then twelve months for progress evaluations. Montgomery agreed.

Each time, they conducted a barometer reading: "Here is what you said you were going to accomplish. Here is where you are at the six-month mark based on feedback that we have gotten from your group, and here is where you are at the twelve-month mark."

For Montgomery, it was good to see some calibration telling them they were on track.

Montgomery was then selected to attend the War College, where he chose a thesis for a research and writing project that eventually became Beyond Words, focusing on what the US Army was getting wrong when it came to leadership.

"We [the army] write a lot of great documents," Montgomery said. "We think we are the best leaders in the world, and we have got some great leadership techniques. But I think we are missing one essential mark, which is we are really not as connected to our people as we should be."

The consequences of this disconnection were devastating. Soldier suicide. Conflicts within families. Conflicts within units. Montgomery knew that the army could get ahead of these issues if leaders were strong enough not to view Tactical Empathy as a touchy-feely technique but a core talent they must comprehend and employ.

The amount of productivity, transparency, honesty, and trust that would permeate throughout the organization "would just be beyond belief, and we were losing that opportunity if we continued to operate as we were."

Notwithstanding, Montgomery continued dealing with nonbelievers.

When he brought the concept of the paper to his staff advisor at the War College, someone who had a background in psychology, he was told, "Bill, I do not see what you are seeing. This is really not gonna make any difference. You are kind of wasting your time while you are here if you are going to put [effort] into this area because the army has already figured this out."

Ironically, as the years wore on, US Army's Training and Doctrine Command (TRADOC) undertook several studies in which they interviewed middle-grade officers and NCOs. Most reported that their leaders were not in touch with their frame of reference, which led to many of them leaving the service.

They would say, "I am passionate about what the army does, but I just cannot operate in an environment where one, my leaders are not authentic and two, I feel like I can do something more than how they are boxing me in at the moment."

Interestingly, the same relational results have been found between coaches and athletes.

ATHLETICS

Bo Hanson understands the importance of putting the needs of people on par with the needs of the organization. Bo is the Director and Senior Coaching Consultant of Athlete Assessments for the University of Technology Sydney in Queensland, Australia. In 1992, he became Australia's youngest rower to compete in the Olympics. He went on to win bronze medals in 1996, 2000, and 2004. Hanson regularly speaks about athlete-centered coaching, leadership, teamwork, and how to use behavioral profiling and EQ to create greater success.

Hanson was fortunate that he had a coach through three Olympics who had a collaborative style. The coach had very specific ideas of how to achieve high performance, yet he also understood the need to engage athletes to keep them involved and contributing to the success of the program.

This collaborative approach involved regular discussions about what worked and what did not and frequent feedback sessions to bounce ideas off one another. They functioned as a cohesive unit, developing trust that lasted for many years.

Hanson said, "If I do not connect with my players, it is a reason for them to potentially leave the program or at least completely disengage from the program. They are seeing now that relationships within the sporting scene are in fact a performance factor. It actually is a competitive advantage."

And for all intents and purposes, it is free. Consider the amount of money that sports spend on facilities, equipment, and travel. "To have a better relationship just takes...well, it just takes empathy, but that is not easy for some coaches to do."

Hanson pointed to the 2008 Summer Olympic Games in Beijing, China. During these Olympics, Canadian athletes won twenty medals, making it the country's second-best nonboycotted Summer Olympics ever, behind the twenty-two they won at Atlanta in 1996. Hanson believes Canada's performance should be attributed to the effective and productive relationship between coach and athlete.

Those who returned with a medal or had personal-best performances (including Ian Miller, who, at age sixty-one and after nine Olympic appearances, won his first medal) did so because of that connection. What does it all mean? It all but confirms the positive relationship an athlete has with their coach is a performance factor. However, this message is only now starting to gain traction within the coaching communities.

Many coaches and leaders make the mistake of failing to put people first. Often coaches come to work with Hanson's groups because their methods to this point have failed. If they do not improve their performance, their job, if not their career, is in jeopardy.

Even after Hanson's counsel, some cannot make the change. For others, the change in their behavior has been significant. They have made the conscious decision to make themselves vulnerable by opening themselves up to their players, and as the student-athletes reciprocate, a closeness develops. It is a new way of thinking and a different way to operate, especially for older coaches. Older coaches did not have coaches who were like that, so they do not have a role model to emulate. That is part of the challenge.

The new generation of athletes, now more than ever, is not interested in dictatorial or autocratic coaching. Hanson recounted a recent conversation with an NCAA Division I basketball coach who said athlete transfer lists are growing astronomically every year as they decide they no longer want to be a part of programs where there is a lack of empathy.

If they do not like something about a program, they do not hang around for the long term as in years past. They look at other options, and rules are being bent or perhaps even rewritten to facilitate this. But Hanson has also worked with programs where the athletes would never transfer out because they feel like they have a deep sense of ownership and belonging in the program. The leaders of these programs adopt the mindset of the primary caregiver. Whether the primary caregiver is a manager, schoolteacher, parent, or coach, to get the best out of the people they are responsible for they need to create an atmosphere where each member actually feels involved and enjoys what they are doing.

Creating an environment where you have highly engaged people is as important in athletics as it is in hostage negotiation. Coaches who engage in HNL principles develop deeper relationships with their athletes and not only influence the athletes in the context of how they perform but actually have a profound impact on their lives.

TAKEAWAYS

- HNL requires that you subordinate yourself to the person you are speaking with in a difficult conversation. This is awkward and counterintuitive, but it pays off.

- Transparency shows you are authentic. The sooner you demonstrate transparency with your direct reports, the sooner they will demonstrate the same with you and others.

- HNL means creating an environment where collaboration and empathy produce a sense of ownership for everyone. Connection and ownership within your teams create an atmosphere where motivation and productivity thrive.

CHAPTER 3

HUMANS OVER EMPLOYEES

PEOPLE OFTEN ASK ME IF HOSTAGE NEGOTIATION IS A SCIENCE or an art. I tell them it is a combination of both but more art than science, and the subject is people.

Hostage Negotiator Leadership challenges us to focus on people first and mission second. With the right implementation, HNL principles can create a collaborative culture where teams see things from various points of view and seek to achieve the best outcome for everyone involved. This people-first mentality has the power to influence everything from daily decision-making to overcoming toxic leadership. It empowers each individual to take ownership of their work and impact.

This is also a model that views leaders as teachers, and the best teachers are those who do not view themselves as superior. Leaders who look down on others tend to create a perception of power that leads to harsh, dismissive, and condescending dynamics with colleagues and customers. Donavan Nelson Butler, Master Sergeant, US Army, was right: "A leader who allows their subordinates to suffer as proof of who is the boss likely quenches their thirst with salt water from a rusted canteen."

Successful leadership, like successful negotiation, demands a human touch that is authentic and uplifting, no matter how challenging the circumstances. When we elevate others, we elevate ourselves and create more opportunities for positive outcomes. When we do not, we suffer the consequences.

PEOPLE, NOT PROBLEMS

Let's take a look at a real-life negotiation where a young man is threatening to commit suicide in his home. He initiates the call to the police from his home. The initiation of the call was a cry for help that he never got.

Call taker: 911 emergency.

Grant: Yeah, uh, the—the police are in front of my house right now.

Call taker: What is your name, sir?

Grant: Grant.

Police officer: Shut up and listen to me. Grant. Grant, shut up and listen to me. Grant. Grant. Grant, people are not being allowed in their house, okay? Are you gonna be a coward?

Grant: You guys have guns pointed at me—

Police officer: Grant, shut up and listen to me. Will you do that? Keep your mouth shut. You need to come out of the house so that other people can go home.

Grant: You can send them home. I am not coming out.

Police officer: Is that right—that they cannot be in their own house because you are being stubborn and being a coward? Instead of being enough of a man to come outside? Answer me, Grant.

Grant: What?

Police officer: Are you gonna be a coward and stay in the house, or are you gonna be a man and come outside and take care of your problems?

Grant was a son, a brother, a human who was screaming for help. The officer saw him as a problem to be solved. It did not end well.

It is ironic to think, but much like this police officer, leaders and managers can forget the people they are responsible for are, in fact, human. Endless spreadsheets, aggregated salaries, calls for service, office expansions, and more can leave us looking at our employees as pieces to be moved around the organizational chessboard.

For HNL it is critical you do not lose sight of the fact your hostage-taker/employee—or in Grant's case, a suicidal man—is, in fact, a human being. The moment you forget the person on the other side of a difficult conversation is human—with all that entails, including negative emotions—is the moment you lose your advantage.

MORE THAN NUMBERS

Natalie Pearson is a data-driven vice president of human relations of a major communications company whose work deserves some careful attention. Described as a dynamic leader with a wealth of experience and insight in strategic decision-making, Pearson is a true teacher who celebrates success and is candid with all levels of feedback.

She is known among peers as having the ability to see things from all sides and work collaboratively to implement HR solutions that support the needs of the business and her customers, the employees. This demands that she evaluates humans as humans instead of just employees or numbers. In other words, she focuses on the "human" in human capital strategies.

Pearson said, "What that means is before I get into, for example, turnover or retention rates, or how we are going to address a diversity and inclusion shortcoming, I take the time to just talk to people. Just understand the history and what you are doing. Ask some questions."

From the C-suite executives to front-line employees, all find it easy relating to Pearson. They find her to be "someone who is easy to build trust in and with and someone they can confide in. I really have focused my energies around mastering the art of HR."

Pearson's approach to HR (note that her area of responsibility is known as human relations, not human resources) is viewing it as an art as opposed to a science. The art is the relational aspect of HR. It is her way of using Tactical Empathy—understanding the psychology of HR as well as people's decision-making skills and capabilities.

She recalled one situation where she used the art of HR as the company was contemplating a reduction in force (RIF). RIFs are largely data driven. The numbers will tell you that you must go from x to y: let's say, for example, from one hundred to eighteen employees. It is pretty cut and dry if you only look at the math. Evaluate the variables. Evaluate the factors. Make your decisions and then execute.

In this particular case, it was not so simple because of the people to be impacted. Looking purely at the data, it made sense that the five people in question needed to go. However, Pearson said, "These were some of our most seasoned professionals who had the history, the context of our operation that the others did not have. And we would have been cutting our nose off to spite our face if we let these particular individuals go."

The C-suite was fully expecting Pearson and her HR team to agree with the list of names that the data supported releasing and make it happen. When analyzing the numbers, Pearson quickly identified the problem (money) and, more importantly, developed a solution.

She said to herself, "There has gotta be another way that we can get to not necessarily the number but the desired savings because at the end of the day it was about productivity and efficiency, which ultimately has cost implications."

She considered a variety of tools, resources, and methodologies the company could modify in lieu of releasing these key individuals. The C-suite was surprised at her recommendations but agreed to implement her suggestions for cost reduction and retain the talent.

Win!

The "art" side of HR also called for Pearson to listen to the C-suite beyond the surface-level things and demonstrate she understood their position, making a point to truly connect with them and view the entire situation globally instead of relying solely on the data.

"It is what it is because the data says this is what we need to do. Well, not all business decisions can be made without incorporating the human element into it," she said.

WHERE THERE IS SMOKE, THERE IS FIRE

Recently, Pearson terminated one of the company directors (I will call him Cody) for his inability to master the company's core competencies, which include building, facilitating, and fostering relationships. No matter how much coaching and training he received over the course of several years, he could not get it right.

Cody was clearly an outstanding functional expert—if not the best, one of the best in the company.

As much as they valued his subject matter expertise, the way he treated his people was abysmal and did not line up with the company's "heart." They had to let him go.

During his exit interview, Cody did not take responsibility for his conduct. It was always someone else's fault. He still did not see any issue with how he led. As disappointing as the loss was, it fell short when compared to the damage he inflicted on his team.

Pearson said, "I was not aware of how damaged they were due to his leadership style, which lacked empathy and emotional intelligence, until he was removed from the organization. So then I had to do an intervention in terms of really reprogramming them and getting them to build their confidence in leadership because he had virtually destroyed it."

Where there is smoke, there is fire. Admittedly, Pearson missed some clues. There had been rumors about Cody's conduct, but Pearson could never corroborate them. She kept a folder regarding the rumors in the hope of someone coming forward with substantial first-person information.

The company has an open-door policy, so any employee can speak to any leader at any time about any issue.

Cody told his team they could not speak to Pearson or her boss without going through him first. Cody had instilled so much fear in his team that no one told Pearson the state of the team—that is, until Marvin announced his retirement.

During his exit interview, Marvin provided information that initiated the investigation that uncovered the depth and breadth of Cody's toxicity. He recalled one meeting wherein Cody introduced a topic with which the majority of the team did not agree. As good teams do, they respectfully but openly voiced their concerns. This embarrassed and angered Cody. His ego and authority saw it as a personal attack.

After the meeting adjourned, he pulled the dissenters into his office one at a time. With each, he closed the door and the blinds and cursed them out.

In another incident, Cody demonstrated micromanaging inclinations so strong that he needed to know where his remote team was and what they were doing at all times.

He would call them and leave voice mail messages. If they did not call him back within minutes—literally minutes—he would call and text them incessantly until they responded. This started at six in the morning and did not stop until nine or ten at night.

To his demise, Cody looked at those under his charge as no more than chess pieces.

HEART COMPANIES

Pearson's company along with Cisco Systems Incorporated, Breakthru Beverage Group, and Ford Motor Company are a few of the companies that emphasize Tactical Empathy in management and product development. All have invested in empathy training to improve management, retain employees, or guide design decisions.

In Pearson's company, the core competencies that got Cody fired are applicable to all midlevel managers up to the C-suite—up and down, horizontally, diagonally, and cross-functionally. Employees are evaluated on how well they engage each other and their employees as well as how they execute and manage change.

The company has an extensive in-house training catalog and provides both online and facilitated training. If any leader falls short in these areas, remedial training or intervention is mandated. Pearson said, "We will literally cast a very exhaustive net before we dismiss a leader based on their lack of EQ, soft skills, or interpersonal skills."

There was no watershed moment that led to the company's stance on Tactical Empathy, EQ, and relationships. This has been a part of their mantra since it was founded over one hundred years ago. For a little context, it is a privately held, family-owned company.

Family-owned businesses can do things that corporations cannot or will not. Families have personalities, and these personalities impact their organizations. When the founder of the company wrote his living will and testament, he included a clause that said that as long as the company is in existence, its first and foremost obligation is to take care of every employee. Not to make money. Not to grow the company by 1,000 percent. To take care of its people.

What does that look like? Pearson's company has had a pension since the company was founded, and they are one of the few that still offers this benefit. When the financial market took a hit and interest rates went into the toilet, they found it increasingly difficult to finance pensions for hundreds of thousands of current and past employees. Financially, the company was starting to go negative.

They reevaluated the portfolio while at the same time remaining true to their belief in taking care of employees. They elected to stop offering the pension to new hires while grandfathering those hired by a certain date. In lieu of pensions for new hires, the company began contributing a 60 percent match of their salary into a 401(k). The new employees had to do nothing. No request. No paperwork. Nothing. The company automatically gave them the money.

Recently the company announced they were shutting down the communications center from which they managed job assignments and dispatched technicians.

All announcements of this type, before they are relayed to the employees, are vetted through HR for feedback and input.

Pearson and her team determined the proposed method of delivery for this message would have been a disaster had it gone out as first suggested. The C-suite believed the employees might walk off after being told they would be losing their jobs, which would have a detrimental effect on work routing not just in Virginia but across the entire company.

To soften the blow, they suggested that HR could buy the affected employees pizza, deliver the news, and provide whatever support they needed. The executives added that if the soon-to-be-fired employees were so emotionally distraught that they could not work, they would be allowed to go home, provided they use their own personal time (accrued leave).

"I cannot think of anything more insulting than, you know, we are going to bring you a pizza as a way of showing our appreciation and thanks for all the years. Some of these folks have been in that department for twenty-plus years. So for all your years of service to the company, here is a slice of Domino's pizza or something. Are you kidding me? Seriously?" Pearson said.

Against the C-suite's direction, Pearson made a conscious decision to treat the employees as she believed they wanted to be treated. After delivering the news, Pearson and her team stayed with them for as long as they wanted, answered every question, and addressed every concern. She vetoed the pizza idea because of the optics. She wanted to be a little classier. She schedule a going-away party for a day other than the one on which they were given notice that they were losing their jobs.

Pearson believes that all leaders need to know their customers to be successful. As mentioned earlier, the employee is the customer in Pearson's line of work. She did not dismiss the C-suite's suggestion because she is a rogue agent, nor does she believe the idea was concocted maliciously. They just did not know her customers as she did and could not appreciate the impact of the message.

"I am obligated to do the right thing by our customer, even if that looks different than a directive from my boss's boss. At the end of the day, we do the right thing by our employees always, and that is kind of how I practice HR."

In this instance, Pearson's way of practicing HR was primarily driven by being sensitive to how decisions and communications impacted her customers.

A TRUE ANALYST

Diane is one of the smartest people Pearson knows. Her intellect makes others around her feel, well, dumb. It is not something she does deliberately. It is almost unconscious.

Diane's attunement to data led to her regularly pointing out mistakes or faulty logic on the part of senior executives. A director in one state highlighting mistakes happening at the C-suite level in another does not go over very well. The senior and executive vice presidents made this abundantly clear to Pearson.

It is true they are primarily a "heart" company, but even in a "heart" company, "head" decisions need to be made. The company needed someone with Diane's skillset. These "head" decisions are made based on data that folks like Diane can analyze and make recommendations about. In short, she was another talent they could not afford to lose; however, the ego and authority of senior executives wanted her out.

Instead of firing Diane, Pearson lowered her profile. She partnered with another leader who appreciated Diane's analytical mind and put her into a completely different function. Now Diane is working outside of the C-suite's line of sight and continues to do amazing work. Pearson again was successful in salvaging the careers of some really good talent.

"For me it was a win in the sense that I did not lose that skillset, which we very much needed, but it was also a challenge because I had to go back and repair some relationships. She had torched some relationships that were key for me to get my business objectives accomplished."

Pearson finds little gratification in accolades and awards. Not to downplay the importance of recognition, but her proudest accomplishments as an HR professional are the teams and leaders she has developed.

"There is one person back in my day at Pizza Hut. He was in operations and I was in HR, and he had a conversation with me.

'Natalie, I really want to get into HR. I do not think I am a fit for operations. How do I do this? How can I enter into your field?'"

Pearson took it as an opportunity to mentor him. He is now the Chief Diversity Officer at Coca-Cola.

"That is what I find rewarding. I attribute my orientation around servant leadership and around team development to those three leaders who showed me that very early on in my career."

TEACHER LEADERS

Retired United States Army Colonel George Reed is the Dean of the School of Public Affairs at the University of Colorado Colorado Springs. He is also a specialist in the study of leadership and ethics. His twenty-seven years of service as an army officer culminated with a professorship as the Director of Command and Leadership Studies at the US Army War College.

In 2003, he and his colleagues were the recipients of a question posed by Secretary of the Army Thomas E. White: "What are we doing to identify, assess, and deal with leaders with a destructive leadership style?" That launched a research project headed up by Reed and Dr. R. Craig Bullis. They gathered a group of senior military officers and asked them the same question of destructive leadership. They were met with many incredible stories of horrible leadership.

"It was like pulling the lid off a can of worms. These very successful, very accomplished officers. The best of the best.

They were going to be the next generation of general officers, telling stories of how they were mistreated along the way by their supervisors. Stories that were completely inconsistent with the world-class military organization. It was really horrific stuff."

Reed knew he and Bullis were on to something and it was incumbent upon them to keep the conversation alive. The result was "Toxic Leadership," published in *Military Review*. However, after its publication, Reed said the only people interested in the conversation were the subordinates who were suffering under it. No senior military leadership. That was then.

Fast-forward to today.

Today's army has 360-degree feedback mechanisms in place. Toxic leadership is a part of the vocabulary. It is taught in all service academies and Reserve Officer Training Corps. The reason it caught on is the midgrade officers who were so interested in toxic leadership in 2003 and 2004 are now senior officers in the top levels of army leadership. While their interest has not waned, progress has been slow.

Reed was often invited to speak at general officer conferences about toxic leadership. Many of the senior officers in attendance would say, "Yeah, George, you are probably right. But, man, it is a whole lot better now than it was fifteen years ago. I mean, fifteen years ago these assholes were all over the place. I could tell you stories that could curl your hair. It is a lot kinder and gentler today."

Reed is a self-described leadership junkie. His "jones" started in the army because, let's face it, the US Army is a wonderful place to study leadership. There are teams within that are identical. Unit A and Unit B can be in the same headquarters. They can be equipped exactly the same. They can be structured exactly the same. The only difference between them is the personalities of their composition and how they are led.

You will not convince Reed that "leadership does not matter because you can walk into Unit A, and everybody is looking down at the ground, and they are all feeling sorry for themselves, and morale is in the tank. You walk next door to Unit B, and everybody is upbeat. They are mission oriented. They are excited to do their job. What is the difference?"

The leader.

Reed was mentored early in his career by leaders who turned working for them every day into a leadership laboratory. They were always experimenting. Always teaching. Always learning.

When he was a lieutenant, one of them told him, "You need to get a leadership notebook. When you find these little tidbits [of advice], you need to put them in a three-ring binder and then open that up from time to time and page through it."

These mentors were instrumental in his leadership development, but he also worked for some who were pretty horrible. The differences always fascinated him. He wondered why the disparity in leadership conduct was seemingly allowed to persist to this degree. How can the soldiers in Unit A suffer under terrible leadership and those in Unit B work under caring, nurturing, developing kinds of leadership within the same organization?

Part of the answer was found in the respected leaders for whom Reed worked. These leaders kept two things top of mind: attention to task and attention to people. It was not always a fifty-fifty proposition. Which one was emphasized changed depending upon the circumstances, but the best leaders always paid attention to both: getting the job done and taking care of your people.

The worst leaders were either all about the mission with no focus on taking care of the people, or they simply were self-absorbed to the point where the only thing they cared about was their professional survival.

LONG-TERM RELATIONSHIPS

Mike Falconer is a former sergeant for a municipal police agency who has maintained several long-term relationships with some of his leaders. This was largely due to their work ethic.

One of his front-line supervisors worked with a level of dedication and task mastery that Falconer could not help but respect. Falconer viewed himself and the supervisor as kindred spirits when it came to their approach to work.

Each of them possessed the desire to pour their heart and soul into any task they undertook, day in and day out. This supervisor was not content with showing up to punch a clock; rather, he came into work to accomplish something. To make a difference. To make things better. To get things done.

Another factor for Falconer that led to long-term connections with his leaders was genuine Tactical Empathy. He would do almost anything for those who displayed it.

One of his best memories of this is one in which he was nearly killed.

Zane Devlin, a high school honor student, sneaked out of his house after midnight to steal a gun from one of two local gun stores. When neither store satisfied him, he started back home at about 1:30 a.m. On the way, he shined a small flashlight into parked cars. In a black duffel bag slung over his shoulder, he carried a crowbar, a pair of black gloves, a small telescope, and a ski mask.

A detective who was on a residential burglary stakeout saw Devlin casing the cars. She contacted Falconer and another plainclothes officer, and they converged on Devlin. In a matter of seconds, while the detective looked through his bag, Devlin, who had the knife clenched in his right hand, punched a uniformed officer in the face.

Falconer and the uniformed officer tackled Devlin. The detective hit Devlin with pepper spray. He flailed about and managed to either slash or stab three of the officers before fleeing. Falconer suffered two stab wounds to the torso.

Thankfully, he survived.

Falconer marveled that both his sergeant and lieutenant visited him at his home as he was recovering. "I genuinely felt they cared about me, and it was beyond, 'I am your boss.' It was, 'I really hope you are okay.' I will always remember that. It was a bad situation, but it was a good memory because it could have gone a completely different way. The things I have seen over time have shown me that was the exception to the rule, unfortunately. That is why, over time, I have appreciated it that much more," he said.

Falconer continued, "If I had issues at home and I brought it to their attention, they got it. They understood and said, 'Okay, that is too bad. I am sorry that is going on,' or they offered their help or their assistance.

"It is genuine because of things that they do and how they do it. They will say, 'Okay. Hey, listen, get out of here a little bit early today. I know you have X, Y, and Z to do.' Or if you are working extremely hard, 'Hey, I know you have been doing a lot. Why don't you take off an hour early?' Or, 'Do you need any help?'"

Falconer called it *credible empathy,* or empathy that was legitimate and genuine about not only what was going on professionally but what was going on with an employee personally.

ILLEGITIMATE PRAISE

Praising employees is a great way to build employee confidence but should be used with caution. Heaping praise on people for doing things that are expected is easily detected and minimizes the significance of legitimately outstanding work.

It lowers the standard of what is excellent.

Giving praise when it is not warranted will have your employees believing that the level of performance being recognized is all that is required to be seen as a high performer. Legitimate high performers will begin to feel as if they are working in a low-performance culture where minimal effort is required for recognition.

When you demonstrate low standards or your praise is not authentic, it diminishes your respect. Eventually, it becomes mere words because your level of recognition does not match reality. If it does not match reality, it loses potency. You lose respect.

Falconer was one of three detectives assigned to high-profile, related murder investigations involving three victims.

One of Falconer's partners, Carlos, was the lead on the most recent homicide in which the suspect knocked on the victim's front door and shot her and her nanny.

Both women were wounded. The nanny survived. The other later succumbed to her injuries. After working tirelessly on the cases for years, Falconer, Carlos, and Sergeant Victor Stevenson closed the case, arrested a suspect, and charged the suspect with the three homicides.

This was huge.

It was a major accomplishment.

Rick, the supervising officer for the three, sought to reward them by inviting them to his home for a dinner party—on its face, a kind gesture. The problem was the dinner was scheduled for a weeknight and only Stevenson lived within twenty minutes' driving distance of Rick's home. Falconer and Carlos were coming from distances that would have taken them well over an hour to arrive. On top of that, they both had toddlers at home.

Falconer was critical of the gesture because it showed a severe lack of understanding of the impact.

"For me to drive all the way out to his house on a Monday night when me and [Carlos] both have kids at our house...to go celebrate with him at his house where it is convenient for him to be is a complete showing that he does not really care."

To Falconer, Rick made the invitation as though it was a box he was checking off. Rick knew he had to do something to acknowledge his guys for closing the case, but the ham-handed way in which it was handled appeared not as a reward but an obligation.

"But he did not see it that way because he did not care. It was obvious that was a shallow attempt to reward me for something that you thought that I did well, but you really did not care. It sticks in my mind that he just did not give a shit, basically. It was almost like he should not even have done it at all. The fact that he even did that made it even worse."

Falconer said he is not looking for constant reinforcement, validation, or praise. He is only looking for it when it is clear he has gone above and beyond what is normally expected of him and the recognition is real.

At his previous agency, praise had become so watered down that people were getting "attaboys" simply for showing up and working their shift. Some people were performing. Some were not. However, leadership viewed all through the same prism. There was no clear delineation between performers and nonperformers.

"I am receiving my outstanding performance award with another detective who everyone in the room knows did not do anything the entire year, who is also getting an outstanding performance award. And I go, 'This officially means nothing now.'"

INSINCERE PRAISE

Prior to working for a rideshare company, Sheri Simpson was working in the States as the centralized monitoring organization lead at Microsoft. The marketing and operations (M&O) lead she worked for was young with no experience in leadership or management. She came to Microsoft with a strong consulting background from PricewaterhouseCoopers.

Simpson said the M&O lead lacked empathy, self-awareness, and self-control. She apparently recognized it as a problem because she was able to feign empathy when it benefited her, as was the case for an upcoming inspection.

Before the inspection, she gave her team personalized cards to tell them how fantastic they were and make them feel appreciated.

After the inspection, the M&O lead got the results that she wanted and resumed her customary effect of not caring about the team.

"Immediately, you know that she is not sincere. We were played as a team—as her team—and it backfired. I left because of her. All my other peers, her direct reports, left because of her. To this day, we thought [she] was a very bad hire, a big, big mistake. We lost talent in that situation."

Insincere praise is just as damaging as no praise at all.

In contrast, Falconer has worked for supervisors who were more sincere in their recognition of a job well done. Amy was one of those supervisors. She would go out of her way to reward her people so that you knew it was unique and specific to the personnel and the job done.

She would say, "'Hey, come in late. Hey, let me take you out to lunch. Hey, let me do this. Hey, here is a gift card for this.' It is always something...that she is going out of her way to make sure that you know she really appreciates what you did. She is a good leader and good supervisor."

Reed agrees. He says the best leaders are great cheerleaders who are always giving credit and always elevating. When leaders do not do it, it is a glaring omission.

Even if they do not engage in otherwise negative behavior, the fact that they are not cheerleading and are not putting their people up for others to see is painfully obvious.

TAKEAWAYS

- Focus on your people first and the mission second. Create a collaborative culture within your teams.

- Implementation is never just about data. It is about people. Incorporate the human element into your decision-making.

- Be a teaching leader. Invest in the growth of your subordinates.

- Be authentic in your praise and concern. This will promote the likelihood of long-term relationships.

CHAPTER 4

TACTICAL EMPATHY

TACTICAL EMPATHY IS THE PURPOSEFUL, DELIBERATE pursuit to accurately recognize and articulate someone else's perspective. In that sense it is different from what we think of as emotional empathy. It is also a key component of the HNL framework and relationship management because everybody feels better when they feel understood.

I have seen this every day in my many years of law enforcement. But teachers, doctors, lawyers, and coaches see it too.

Tactical Empathy is a term coined by the Black Swan Group to define the deliberate drive to accurately recognize and articulate another's emotional state or perspective so well that you could summarize it for them. The best purveyors of this type of empathy are therapists, hostage negotiators, and sociopaths. All three use it, not because we are necessarily nice people but because it works.

Tactical Empathy should not be confused with emotional empathy, which is a subjective state brought on by emotions. Emotional empathy is our automatic drive to respond appropriately to another's emotions. For example, if someone starts to tell me a story about how they lost their pet and they start to tear up, I too will get a lump in my throat because it is sad to see someone wrestling with that kind of pain.

Tactical Empathy takes conscious effort but also is very similar to intuition. Your gut is telling you this is how they see things, but intuition is not enough. If you do not vocalize it, it matters not. Articulating what you are seeing or hearing is where most people struggle.

I have had great success with it in the world of hostage negotiations, in which we are navigating highly emotional situations where logic and reason are scarce. Similarly, the negative responses you get from your employees often come from an illogical place based primarily on emotion. They will not make sense to you, and they do not have to.

Viewing the world through the eyes of the hostage-taker—or in your case, the employee—allows you to perceive the meaning and motivations behind their behavior as well as the emotions attached to them. You do not necessarily need to get it right. You just need to make an honest *attempt* to get it right.

People love to have other people understand how they feel.

LACK OF SUPPORT

Harald Jahrling is a famous Australian crew coach who once said, "I don't believe in sport as a democracy. Sport is a dictatorship."

Sally Robbins rowed for Jahrling, and pushing herself beyond her physical capabilities caused her dramatic meltdown during the 2004 Athens Olympic final. It is still described as one of the most devastating moments in Australian

Olympic history, the moment she stopped rowing in the women's eight finals, suffering a psychological breakdown.

"Suddenly fatigue sets in, and I just cannot move, you know? It is a feeling of paralysis where you just hit the wall."

It does not get much worse than that in rowing, a sport that requires fluid and persistent motion. Just stopping is the ultimate contradiction. You just do not do it.

Robbins's issue was not a secret. She had a history of stoppages that teammates knew about.

Captain Julia Wilson: "I think everybody in Australian rowing knew about it. Whether they say they did or they didn't, I think everybody knew."

Teammate Kyeema Doyle: "It was there, but no one talked about it. And to compete to your best ability at a World Cup or a world championships or an Olympics, you can't spend any time thinking about anyone else."

Teammate Jodi Winter: "Just occasionally you couldn't help but think something would spark off about Sally's past or, 'I wonder if it's going to happen again.' And it's something you didn't want to think about."

As author Peter Wilkins wrote in *Don't Rock the Boat*, "It was stunning to find out that there had been so many times where this sort of flaw had surfaced and yet nothing had been done about it. How could this be? How could a rower keep on rowing in a team sport where one of the main priorities, one of the main criteria is the ability to row from point A to point B? From a little bit of digging there was evidence, anecdotally and otherwise, that it had happened possibly as many as nine times before."

Harald Jahrling supposedly said at the time, "I have dealt with that." Fully aware of Robbins's plight, he selected her for the team anyway.

It is a classic example of ego and authority leading to an unhealthy outcome.

It was not just the selection of Robbins that damaged the relationships within the boat. It was Jahrling's commanding and controlling style. He demanded that the crew operate within a very rigid structure where they were rowing three days on, one day off, keeping them out of sync with the rest of the world. Instead of having a weekend where they could socialize and have relationships outside of the sport, they were locked in with each other for the sake of the boat.

"You ate, slept, and rowed, and that was it. It was horrible," Doyle said. "Looking back on it, I don't know how I did it."

Robbins quitting midrace proved to be a horrible result. The team got to the finish with only seven people pulling the boat over the line, dead last, in front of the world. It was the biggest moment in Robbins's life and her worst performance ever. The team was racked with anger, frustration, and disappointment. Emotionally, they were devastated.

Was Jahrling there at the pontoon to see them come in and console them? No. According to many accounts, he vacated the facility, leaving the athletes he was responsible for to process what had just occurred on their own.

Many of them never got over it—not just that Robbins had stopped rowing but also that Jahrling had abandoned them. A coach has a responsibility to display Tactical Empathy so that if an athlete or team has a bad performance, the coach is there to provide support. The coach has to be the person to manage the conversation about what happened and the emotions associated with it.

From his perspective as a rower and a coach, Hanson said, "For him not to even be there...it's almost criminal."

For his part, Jahrling said he regretted failing to stay by their side and deal with the issue immediately, but he also blamed the Australian authorities for failing to ask him to come back and address the reactions to the team's performance. When the issue was addressed further, it was suggested that Jahrling caught a flight out of Athens while the team was still "screaming and wailing."

To this day, Jahrling is unapologetic about his overall leadership style, which is ego-dominant and authoritative. "I'm a total control freak. You can't get world-class performances if you just let everyone loose everywhere. Someone's got to be a dictator." Jahrling is still involved with the sport. He returned to Australian Row in 2016 as a "key strategist."

This is far too common. Leaders who behave extremely poorly often slip under the radar for a period of time and then resurface somewhere else, leaving a trail of broken employees and organizations in their wake.

Many athletes finish their careers emotionally scarred because of their relationships with their coaches. These coaches harassed, bullied, or communicated with the athletes in a negative fashion. There is a fundamental deficiency in their ability to demonstrate Tactical Empathy and create a safe environment for their athletes—physically, emotionally, and psychologically.

Plenty of examples come out of US colleges every year.

Alexander Wolfe wrote a piece a few years back for *Sports Illustrated* where he documented abusive NCAA coaches. Wolfe noted college sports has a long tradition of coaches engaging in conduct "that would meet most modern tests of torture." Hyperbole? Maybe, but I got his point. He said the behavior is surfacing with more frequency now because players, empowered by today's technologies, are no longer rolling over and taking it.

While there are examples of physical abuse—former Indiana basketball coach Bobby Knight head-butting Sherron Wilkerson during a game in 1994 comes to mind—most of today's abuse is not physical but psychological or emotional. In one study, 41 percent of athletes reported being so depressed it was difficult to function.

Jim Thompson founded Positive Coaching Alliance (PCA), a San Francisco Bay-area group that focuses on mitigating the negative coaching paradigm. As he puts it, "It's hard to be driven when you're being driven. The best way to get the best out of athletes is to create a positive culture in which they're respected and believe in their value and that the coach believes in them."

The "my way or highway" coach with an elevated ego and authority has historically been the norm. However, there is abundant research showing that this is not the best way to increase performance.

Surprisingly, the problem of abusive coaches may be greater with coaches of nonrevenue sports than with the larger football or basketball programs.

David Jones, who has covered Penn State athletics for more than two decades, wrote, "The actions of unscrupulous non-revenue coaches often fly under the radar. Their sports are off on their own, watched and attended mainly by the friends and families of the athletes. What they say and do at practice and even during games is easily overlooked by the mass audience of sport. Few take notice of how they behave. So they can get away with all sorts of conduct high-profile coaches cannot."

This is where consultants like Hanson have so much wisdom to share: "Sport is played by people, coached by people, and managed by people, so it is imperative to get the people side right. And business is no different!"

In addition to working with athletes, he works with corporations. The corporations usually give Hanson six months to work with a leader in order to facilitate positive change. He coaches people to work together in answering several key questions. How do you start demonstrating more Tactical Empathy toward others? How does Tactical Empathy defuse negativity? How does Tactical Empathy engage people?

BE LIKE WATER, MAKE FRIENDS

Devin Singh, Assistant Professor of Religion at Dartmouth College, teaches courses on ethics, social capital, and the connections between religion, economics, and politics. His self-described "side hustle" is working for a strategic business advisory firm that focuses on creating high-performing culture rooted in trust, communication, and collaboration.

Singh is developing work in emotional and cultural intelligence as it applies to organizations. Through his work, he has learned that in many cases, well after their careers have started, today's leaders come to the revelation that something is missing.

Empathy.

There is an emptiness and a longing for a deeper, richer sense of character related to empathy that they have never been told how to develop or demonstrate. He has often pondered what it might look like to come into a corporate, government, law enforcement, military, or athletic environment with training on how to build and maintain quality relationships. Similar to Simpson, he asks how the message can be conveyed that this is as valuable as any "hard" skill.

By changing thought processes and behavior.

But why would a leader change? Professor Singh says, "You have to have a reason to change. You have to be motivated. You also have to know how to change. You have to know when it is time for you to change. There are times when a leader's whole philosophy has to change." It is not about turning them into different people. It is about changing behaviors that alienate people. Failure to do so is an expensive proposition.

"There is a way in which a certain level of care and concern and connection is pretty necessary—pretty fundamental in order for authentic communication to happen, in order for teaching and learning to take place, in order for a vision to be persuasive to others and get that buy-in and participation."

An avid martial artist, Singh believes most martial arts, at least in their traditional forms, are about the pursuit of self-discipline, self-control, composure, calmness in the face of adversity, and ultimately trying to avoid violent conflict. This is where martial arts and Tactical Empathy connect. It is not about avoiding confrontation or conflict but rather "how to confront and do conflict well." In other words, it is cultivating EQ.

"A lot of martial arts traditions will advocate things like self-awareness—being aware of your emotions. Being aware of your stress levels. Being aware of your anxiety and how you might uncritically react and respond to something. So for me, there's a real clear connection."

Martial arts icon Bruce Lee once said, "Be like water making its way through cracks. Do not be assertive, but adjust to the object, and you shall find a way around or through it. If nothing within you stays rigid, outward things will disclose themselves. Empty your mind, be formless. Shapeless, like water. If you put water into a cup, it becomes the cup. You put water into a bottle and it becomes the bottle. You put it in a teapot, it becomes the teapot. Now, water can flow or it can crash. Be water, my friend."

It speaks to the adaptability, flexibility, and strength that you achieve with Tactical Empathy.

Remaining composed during an attack is of vital importance. I call it "staying in your seat." An attack in the Tactical Empathy sense can be as intense as an ad hominem, emotion-laden attack or as mild as pushback or passive-aggressive conduct.

Maintaining your composure starts with interrupting that automatic or unconscious response to a literal or figurative attack. Many people use the attack as a manipulative tool because they know they will get one of two responses. You will attack back (fight), or you will compromise your position (flee) because you are uncomfortable. Both are emotional responses, and as stated, emotions impede rationale. Tactical Empathy provides a third option: make friends.

In martial arts, a sense of confidence and strength comes from having a specific skillset that might be needed for a certain situation. The same thing can be said for a leader versed in Tactical Empathy. With it, you know you have the ability needed to make hard decisions, influence, convey bad news, lead your people through difficult times, and maintain relationships.

TOP TO BOTTOM

Simpson, who I highlighted above, promotes a clear vision of Tactical Empathy for her teams, encouraging them to be authentic and empathetic with one another. She ensures everyone on her team feels they have a mentor they can trust and believes in collaborating across teams to drive efficiency and scale for success.

In her twenty years of working for large, international companies, Simpson has used Tactical Empathy to navigate the workplace, winning her "the trust, the heart, and the love of people." The importance of "dialing up" EQ was revealed to her during her time in the highly political and competitive environment at Google.

There, many of the top "leads" were busy making sure that they stayed at the top at the expense of others. Simpson obliged herself to protecting her team and making sure they could function without disruption, distraction, or harassment from those clawing their way up. Using Tactical Empathy, she managed relationships with those who had C-suite aspirations. Like Pearson, she showed she understood what they were trying to accomplish while staying attuned to the needs of her team.

"In a way, I'm directly negotiating with a senior management, saying, 'Look, guys. I'll do my part. I'll be a really good right hand to you. Just give me all the support that I can have, and don't disturb my team.'"

Simpson showed her executives that she understood where they were coming from and was trying her best to support them. Her goal was to ensure the mission was accomplished and the executives looked good doing it.

As a leader, Sheri Simpson has an uncanny acumen for Tactical Empathy.

THE BIRTH OF TACTICAL EMPATHY

Active listening skills (ALS) are the foundation upon which Tactical Empathy is built. ALS was introduced by clinical psychologist and psychotherapist Carl Rogers in the 1950s. They were adopted for use in law enforcement in the mid-1980s and have seen increased use in the business world since the mid-2000s.

The adoption by law enforcement came as a result of our recognizing that regardless of the type of hostage-taker we were dealing with—criminal, crazy, or crusader—they all are operating under stress, which induces a crisis state of varying degrees. Borrowing techniques from a psychotherapist seemed to be the right move. Since that time, it has proven, in terms of lives saved, to be the most effective tool we have ever developed...er, stolen.

Tactical Empathy involves you gathering information. Once you have gathered information about the other person's motivations and show that you understand their current state, you have built rapport. Rapport leads you to trust-based influence, and then you can get to your objective, your case in chief, or your ask. Many times, we get it backward. We want to begin the conversation by stating our objective, and then we are baffled when we get pushback.

My objective as a hostage negotiator was to get the bad guy to release the hostages and surrender. You know that. I know that. Taken out of the circumstance, the hostage-taker knows that. That being the case, how often do you think I picked up the phone, called into the crisis site, and said to the bad guy, "It is Derek from the police department. Since my objective is to get everyone out safe, why not put your gun down, let those people go, and come on out?"

The answer is never! But why? After all, that is my ultimate objective, so why did I not lead with that?

First, they are operating at an intense emotional level in response to a highly stressful event. When emotions are high, rational thinking is low. You cannot begin to direct someone's decision-making until you address the emotional aspects as they see them.

Second, the sequencing is wrong. The sequence is Tactical Empathy first, objective last. As Dana did with Mike in Chapter 3, it is all about understanding the human-nature response and subordinating yourself. Then it is on to your objective.

Once you understand human nature—i.e., what motivates them, what they value, who they have to influence, and the circumstances they are in—that person ultimately becomes predictable because you have a full appreciation of where they are coming from.

Leaders who display Tactical Empathy are assets to their organizations, in part because they are able to effectively build and maintain relationships, and they understand it is not about them.

TAKEAWAYS

- Tactical Empathy is not emotional empathy. It is the purposeful, deliberate ability to accurately recognize and articulate another's perspective.

- People love to have others understand what they are going through.

- Sequencing is important. The sequence is Tactical Empathy first, objective last. It is all about subordinating yourself and understanding the human-nature response.

- Lack of Tactical Empathy has a dramatic effect on individuals, teams, and businesses.

CHAPTER 5

INCLUSION

INCLUSION IS ABOUT EMPOWERING PEOPLE. AS LEADERS WE
need to encourage smart, capable people to bring their best
to our organizations. But when we let ego and authority take
over, we are likely to make unilateral decisions that are not
people-driven. That model of leadership, creating an environment where the leaders are unapproachable, is a thing
of the past.

We need to value others and show them how much they
matter to our organizations. An inclusive culture can manage
any conflict or difficult conversation with transparency that
builds trust and strengthens your mission. This kind of culture
that celebrates people and rewards their good work does not
have to compromise objective standards.

Inclusion requires listening with Tactical Empathy, which
builds habits around respect and humility.

The worst thing you can do is bring intelligent, capable
people onto your teams and then treat them like you cannot
trust them to make decisions or execute without you hovering
over them.

Select them and train them, and then get out of their way.

LET THEM DO THEIR JOB

Leaders need to model the values of their organizations in ways that encourage inclusive behavior. This means inspiring others to collaborate and work together, ensuring everyone is heard and ideas are shared.
—LYNNE DOUGHTIE

Cameron Smith left the community mental health center in an agitated state. Concerned, one of the clinical social workers called the police to conduct a "welfare check" at Cameron's home. Police arrived at his home and saw his Ford Explorer parked in the driveway. The truck looked as if it had been struck multiple times on the hood with an ax.

Police knocked on the door but got no answer. One of the officers walked to the east side of the house to peer in a window and found himself face-to-face with Cameron, who was looking out of the same window, ax on his shoulder as if it were a rifle.

"Open the door, Cameron," the officer said.

Cameron shook his head and said, "Come in and get me. I got something for you."

Two of my best negotiators and I were the first HNT members to arrive on the scene. Jill and Sandy would be making contact with Cameron. Jill was the primary, and Sandy was her coach.

Jill and I came on the team at the same time in 1997, and Sandy joined a few years later. Both were empowered with managing the conversation as they saw fit. I was just there to keep them as distraction-free as possible and organize the responding resources for what had the makings of an extended barricade.

They were about fifty yards from me, in contact via radio.

Sandy said, "He is talking to Jill from the window. He says he wants to finish his peanut butter sandwich and lemonade. The dialogue is good but I need you to get her out of here."

"Her" was a patrol sergeant, standing right behind Sandy, offering suggestions about things in which she was not trained. It was becoming a distraction for both Jill and Sandy. I took care of "her."

Sandy knew her job and thus kept me updated on the dialogue I was unable to hear, so I felt no need to inundate her with a bunch of questions.

Sandy said, "She is locked in with him pretty good. He is pissed at the people down at mental health."

After about thirty minutes of negotiations, Sandy said, "He said he finished the sandwich and lemonade, but he still is not ready to come out...wait...now he says he is ready, but he wants two things. He wants to brush his teeth, and he wants to surrender directly to Jill. He wants her to cuff him."

Now if you had asked me prior to this incident if I would ever let the bad guy surrender directly to my primary negotiator, I would have told you no. I was trained to never allow a primary to directly accept the surrender of the bad guy, for safety reasons.

Sandy was in essence saying, "Hey, boss, I know what you are gonna think but..."

I said, "What are your thoughts on it?"

Sandy said, "Hold on a sec. Okay. Stafford [the SWAT sergeant] said if we can get him out with no shirt on, his hands over his head, we can walk him out to the middle of the street and prone him out, facing away from us. At that point, Jill can go out and cuff him. He said that they (SWAT) will cover down until the cuffs are on."

I said, "Is Jill good with that?"

I could see Jill nod her head indicating that she had heard my query over the radio. Stafford, too, gave the thumbs-up in my direction.

So I said, "Let's do it."

By this time, we were in the process of obtaining a mental temporary detention order (TDO) for Cameron. Murdering your own car is not a crime; however, Cameron's behavior was clearly a danger to himself and the community. The TDO was necessary for us to have the lawful authority to take him into custody so he could get the services he needed.

Jill gave Cameron the instructions, and he appeared in the doorway, hands empty, no shirt. He raised his hands high above his head and walked down the steps of the front porch, looking to the left and the right. At this point there were no fewer than six rifles, handguns, shotguns, and less-lethal weapons pointed at him.

He continued into the middle of the street, hands above his head, and turned all the way around to face the house. He then knelt in the street, one knee at a time. Jill told him to lie facedown.

"Fuck that," he said.

Jill said okay but told him not to move. She exchanged

looks with Stafford, and he nodded. Jill walked to the middle of the street and handcuffed Cameron.

I could have overridden the decision on the surrender. But what would that have said to Sandy and Jill? That I did not trust them. It would have been offensive to both. Probably more so to Jill.

Remember, she came on the team with me. Hell, she came on the department with me. We spent the better part of our work lives together for twenty years. She knew as much if not more than I did. If I had said no to the surrender because it did not fall in line with what we always did, it could have done serious damage to our relationship.

NEW IDEAS AND OPINIONS

Not asking for or refusing to take input is a quick way to create robotic employees who do not believe they have the authority to offer up opinions, ideas, or suggestions.

Encourage your team to speak their mind no matter how outlandish. With my team, I established early that new ideas and opinions were expected.

During these hostage-taking events, I engage the team in "time-outs," intentional or unintentional breaks in the conversation with the bad guy where we can come together and brainstorm. Basically, we strategize about where we were, where we are, and where we would like to go. Everyone on the team, not just those in direct contact with the hostage-taker or barricaded person, is allowed to share thoughts, suggestions, and questions.

I constantly remind the team that our brainstorming sessions are a time for candid talk and the expectation is that all contribute. No topic is forbidden. Some ideas raise eyebrows from time to time, but no idea is stupid.

If they have a problem with what we are doing in pursuit of a successful resolution of the incident, the time to learn that is not after the incident is over. It does us no good then. I need to know in the moment because it could have an effect, positive or negative, on the incident.

While I still have the final say-so, they are encouraged to use their knowledge, skills, and abilities to influence my decision. This is what Sandy and Jill did in Cameron's case.

It is the same approach used in Bo Hanson's athlete-centered coaching philosophy. Hanson says that if you do not believe your athletes have any right to make decisions, you will not be on board with anything he teaches. Most coaches believe in giving athletes some decision-making leeway, but it is closely managed. This is problematic when you put them out on the court or field, under pressure to perform, and something is not working.

They cannot be expected to make decisions to change the course of events because they have not been conditioned to make them autonomously. They will wait for the coach's instructions. A large part of the philosophy for coaches and athletes is to create environments where athletes are encouraged to make decisions free from negative repercussions.

The positive effects can even be seen in theaters of war.

Remember Colonel Montgomery? When he was a middle-grade captain, he deployed with his unit for the first time in Operation Desert Shield, the United States' response to Iraq's invasion of Kuwait on August 2, 1990.

The colonel and his soldiers became part of an international coalition in the war against Iraq that would be launched as Operation Desert Storm five months later. At the time Montgomery was assigned to the Twenty-Fourth Infantry Division at Fort Stewart, Georgia. He was the company commander, in charge of about 180 people in an infantry division of 17,000.

They had just been alerted to the deployment, and many of his soldiers were uneasy.

As they were preparing to leave, Montgomery recalls his soldiers asking, "Hey, sir, what is the big picture? We see what is happening in front of us right now, and we are trying to get our arms around it, but we do not see what is outside our company at the battalion and division level. What is really going on?"

Military experts were portraying any armed engagement with Iraq as a potential bloodbath, which did not help his company from a psychological standpoint. The battalion commander's lack of Tactical Empathy did not help either. His attitude was, "Do what I say, without question. I really do not have time to listen to you because you are younger and do not have the experience. You just need to move out."

He was insensitive to the soldiers' angst and made no attempt to connect with them. He demonstrated little interest in their need for clarification. The silver lining to the battalion commander's behavior was Montgomery and the other three company commanders began to bond more closely before they ever crossed the border into Iraq.

They started to protect each other. They started to share with each other. They actually started to mentor each other as opposed to turning to the battalion commander.

Montgomery remembered a time just prior to the invasion when all four of them met at some hole-in-the-wall Bedouin tent that sold chickens in the desert of Saudi Arabia. As they sat in the tent, they commiserated about their boss. They asked each other, "Well, how are we going to deal with this? We do not need to take the toxicity this guy is putting out and bring it down to our own units. We basically need to figure out how we can make some good of it."

This particular battalion commander was on one side of the spectrum. At the other end of the spectrum was General Barry McCaffrey. At the time McCaffrey was a two-star general and Montgomery's division commander.

Montgomery's specialty when he was in theater was communications.

McCaffrey spent a lot of time with the communicators in the Tactical Operations Center (TOC) because he wanted to stay abreast of the communications networks, taking particular interest in their flexibility and redundancy. He wanted this level of oversight because he understood if they did not have a robust communications plan, both Desert Shield and Desert Storm were doomed to failure.

McCaffrey made sure to include the company commanders (including Montgomery) at the table when he was talking to the battalion commander each week. Montgomery and his peers knew at least once a week they were going to get a small dose of quality leadership from the senior boss, and they loved it.

They felt empowered because they were being asked for input from a two-star general about something of vital importance to the overall war plan.

It made Montgomery's job easier because it was clear that McCaffrey understood exactly what his soldiers needed. As a result, he ended up being a de facto mentor to the four company commanders. When the battalion commander dispensed his very narrow and direct type of leadership, McCaffrey would immediately say, "Okay, thanks, Dennis. I appreciate that, but that is not what we are going to do."

McCaffrey did it in a way that he was not demeaning to the battalion commander, even though Montgomery could sense their relationship was not the best.

McCaffrey was a master at people connection.

McCaffrey walked up to the acetate board, transferred his thoughts to script, and said, "I think this is going to work a lot better, based on what I have seen of the battlefield." He then looked at Montgomery and his peers and asked, "You guys got this?"

To Montgomery, McCaffrey showed he understood that "if you are going into a battle or some type of a conflict, the more transparency and trust that you get from the people you are communicating with to help you with your operation, the better prepared you are going to be when things actually happen."

MEN AND WOMEN

When my HNT was at full strength, I had fourteen negotiators under my charge. Of those fourteen, the top three, as far as the ability to engage someone in crisis, were women. Some of the most productive coaching clients I have engaged have been women.

When asked about her most inclusive leader, Sheri Simpson recalled Taylor Black, who she said had the highest EQ and understanding of Tactical Empathy of anyone for whom she had ever worked.

Black and Simpson would often take five-minute "walk and talks," discussing everything under the sun, but mostly what was going on with Simpson. Whenever Black gave her an assignment he knew she would find difficult, he would apologize. Black was always concerned about Simpson, especially when he put her into a tough spot as was the case with her first assignment to the rideshare team in Malaysia.

The most powerful product of Tactical Empathy is reciprocity. Show it first, and it returns to you. "The first thing he said was, 'I am sorry you have to go through this, Sheri.' I responded to him, 'You know, Taylor, all of us are going through this, and I am sorry you have to be in this situation as well.'"

Simpson said because Black tactically empathized with her, she felt compelled to show Tactical Empathy toward him. She added, "To me he is real. He is human, and that resonates well with me. He was one true leader I felt I could trust. He would tell me he understood what, where, and why I was going through this. He gave me the autonomy and empowerment to do what I had to do...that also he needed my help with general managing. He was all about understanding my emotional state, what I was going through, the stress I was going through, and gave me that support. Because of that I would die for him."

Black's successor was the polar opposite. This guy came from a global investment banking firm and was the consummate corporate player. He had no use for EQ or Tactical Empathy.

Because of this, the team felt disconnected from him and viewed him as unapproachable. Simpson said that he was more representative of the men in her space.

Colonel Montgomery learned a valuable lesson on men, women, and Tactical Empathy while working on his master's degree in human resources from the University of Oklahoma. On his list of required reading was *You Just Don't Understand: Women and Men in Conversation,* authored by Deborah Tannen.

The thesis of the book, according to Montgomery, is men know men, but they really do not know women as much as they think they do. On the other side of the coin, women know women and probably know men better than men know women.

She opines the more you know about the other gender, the better you will be able to manage conflict, and the better you will be able to connect and use resources that you probably did not know were available.

He said, "I know as men we tend to be wired to want to fix things and solve problems ahead of listening to somebody talk to us. I would come home as a newly married guy with two kids, and my wife would begin to tell me challenges she had with the kids while I was away doing my army thing.

"As soon as I heard the problems, what did I do? I started to say, 'Well, did you try this? Why did you not do that?' Eventually, after she put up with that for several months, she looked at me and said, 'Bill, if you would have only listened to the rest of my story, you would have heard that I already solved the problem, but you were so quick to make your comments that you did not even listen to me.'"

As a leader, this conversation with his wife of twenty-five years stunned him. He thought that if he was doing this to his wife, there was a good chance he was doing it with the personnel he was supposed to be supporting.

If that is true, he wondered, "What am I missing?"

Tannen notes that women seek connection, while men seek status. Each seeks more than that, but these contribute to the differences in how men and women communicate.

She continues by highlighting that women will listen just to create empathy. They will listen attentively for a long period without interrupting. When they do interrupt, it is to show support or to ask questions for clarity.

Men, on the other hand, have a tendency to interrupt in order to grab attention and demonstrate how smart they are. They are often inclined to avoid asking questions because they believe it exposes weaknesses and gives control of the conversation back to someone else.

As soon as Montgomery read Tannen, he changed the way he came home from "doing his army thing." He told his wife he recognized he had not shown her that he understood what she had gone through during the day. He was too focused on what was going on in his head.

He began inviting her to share what her gut was telling her about whatever the issue was, even if it was 180 degrees opposite of his thinking. The change in his behavior made a difference. She began to share options, alternatives, and ideas with him that he had not considered.

Had they stayed on the same track as before, it would have taken a toll on their relationship. His encouragement for her to share benefited the family unit. Likewise, the same type of encouragement will benefit your organization.

SIR, THAT IS BULLSHIT!

Colonel Reed, who I highlighted before, identified a leader under whom he worked multiple times throughout his career. He enjoyed working for him so much that he actually sought him out. Whenever he moved to a new position, Reed tried to follow. At the time, Reed was a lieutenant, and his boss was the "enlightened" major.

The major was influential because he was positive. How could it be that in an organization like the US Army, some leaders were just excited to get up and go to work at four in the morning while others dreaded it?

The "enlightened" major was the former. He had a sense of humor and would mess with Reed in a developmental way. It was fun for Reed to come to work because he knew his major had his best interests at heart.

Prior to working for the "enlightened" major, Reed was very anxious about doing the right things. He wanted to do well without knowing what that really meant. He had no one to show him. He was working for a boss whom he called the "Lister."

He and Reed would meet in the morning, at which time he would give Reed a list of thirty-five things to complete. Reed would run around for most of the morning, trying to complete all thirty-five. They would then meet for lunch, where the major would give him another list.

This went on for about nine or ten months.

Reed is an ideas guy—a consummate thinker who every now and again comes up with something brilliant. During one of the interactions with the Lister, Reed said, "Hey, boss. I have got an idea."

The Lister said, "Ah, ah, ah. Stop. Stop. I am not paying you to have ideas. I am paying you to do what the hell I tell you to do." The Lister was not a bad person. He was just more task-oriented than relationship-oriented, and very focused on his own aspirations.

Fortunately for Reed, the Lister eventually moved on and was replaced by the "enlightened" major.

One day, Reed was summoned to the major's office after he had been at the helm for a few weeks. "George," he said, "I want you to do X, Y, and Z."

Reed replied, "Yes, sir," spun on his heels, and started to leave.

The major stopped him. "George? What I just asked you to do, did that sound like the right thing?"

Reed was confused and told the major as much. The major responded, "Well, let me put it this way. What I asked you to do...was there anything in there that you thought was stupid?"

Still not understanding what the major was driving at, Reed said, "Hey, you are the boss."

The major, chagrined, said, "No, no, no! It is not your job to run off and do stupid shit that I tell you to do. It is your job to turn around and tell me it is stupid. So now we are gonna rehearse. Look me in the eye and say, 'Sir, that is bullshit.'"

Before long they were both standing in the office, slamming their fists down on the table together over and over while screaming, "Sir, that is bullshit!" at each other.

The major explained that was what he wanted from Reed anytime he gave him an order or made a suggestion that did not make sense. He said, "If I tell you to do something that is off, you gotta fire it back at me."

Two weeks later, Reed was walking by the same office and the colonel—a.k.a. the big boss—was in with the major. As the major saw Reed pass, he said, "George, come in. I could use your advice."

"You see what he did right there? That, in and of itself, was pretty darned cool. I was a lieutenant. 'George, I need your advice.' He is telling his boss's boss that I am a person whose advice he appreciates. He is cheerleading right off the bat."

Reed entered the office. The major began telling Reed about the son of a sergeant-major who had been stopped eleven times by the military police, and the sergeant-major was convinced the police were targeting his kid. The plan they were contemplating was to flag the kid's license plate so that an alert would be generated, instructing the user to notify the duty officer, who would in turn determine if the stop was valid.

When Reed heard the plan, he balled up his fist and slammed it in the middle of the table, looked the major right in the eye, and said, "Sir, that is bullshit."

The colonel, who was not in on the game, jumped up from the couch and lunged at Reed.

"He was ready to tear my face off. My boss threw his body in between me and the colonel and said, 'No, sir. No, sir. This is good. This is good, We have been working on this.'"

The major explained what he had instructed Reed to do and then turned to Reed and said, "Now get the hell out of here before he kills you."

That was the kind of environment he was creating all the time, and Reed loved it.

The major was not this way with just Reed. He was consistent with all under his charge. There was no favoritism. He genuinely cared about each of them and their growth. He was always teaching, and they were always learning.

"It was just a wonderful relationship. He is in a small group of people that if he called me up tomorrow and said, 'Look, we are gonna assault the gates of Hell. Are you in?' because he was the one who asked me, I would be in. That is how tight that gets. There is very little he can ask of me that I would not do unless it was illegal. He was the exception, on the positive side."

The major was nurturing without compromising his task-oriented nature or high standards. He was demanding and challenging. He pushed his people to excel, and they felt that push. They knew he was 100 percent invested in them and would do almost anything for them. It was a two-way street. The best leaders recognize empathy begets empathy.

RESPECT, HUMILITY, TRUST

General Martin Dempsey was the Chairman of the Joint Chiefs of Staff from 2011 to 2015. After retirement he wrote a book called *Radical Inclusion*, which described the leadership lessons he learned through the challenges of the post-9/11 years.

Dempsey says, "If you're a leader, you must commit yourself to learning. And if you really commit yourself to that, you can't simply be satisfied with reinforcing what you already know. You have to stretch yourself out in order to truly learn, which allows you to do what's most important as a leader today—be a sense-maker for those who follow you."

Effective leaders listen. Listening with Tactical Empathy, they learn by showing respect. Dempsey says any meaningful relationship, and any effective collaboration, starts with respect.

Respect is fed by humility. Humility breeds trust. When people trust you, they will work with you. If they trust you, they will do almost anything for you because you are humble, approachable, and transparent.

Yes, leaders should be ambitious, confident, and mission-oriented. But they need to balance those drivers with doing what is best for their people and the organization. Good leaders tamp down their personal ambitions and consider gaining others' trust first.

Any time you get pushback, dissension, or a no, it is largely due to trust issues.

Finally, Dempsey says the best leaders not only seek but depend on counsel and input from those they lead. This inclusiveness allows them to effectively manage crisis and uncertainty.

Inclusive leaders simply make better decisions.

TAKEAWAYS

- Do not discourage smart, capable people within your organization by not inviting input. Do not let your ego and authority make you feel that you need to make unilateral decisions on every single issue.

- Even in the military, the "do what I say, without question" style of leadership is dying.

- Include your direct reports in information sharing. Show them that you value their insight.

- In any conflict or difficult conversation, the more transparency and trust you show, the quicker you can accomplish your mission.

- Be a cheerleader for your people. Legitimately promote and reward their good work.

- You can be nurturing without compromising objective standards. You can be demanding and challenging as long as your people know you are invested in them.

- Listening with Tactical Empathy means you are learning.

- Tactical Empathy is the manifestation of respect, humility, and inclusivity.

PART II

EGO AND AUTHORITY

CHAPTER 6

THE ACTION IMPERATIVE

IT TAKES REAL COMMITMENT AND DISCIPLINE TO LEAD WITH the HNL model.

The ego and authority model is so common that it is hard to break away from the negative influences it has on our decision-making in everyday life and high-stakes situations. Cultures that prioritize ego and authority often lead to micromanagement of subordinates, who need our trust to truly flourish.

Leaders who build trust are leaders who inspire action. The more trust you can establish, the more confidently you and your team will be able to assess risk, determine the best process, and make hard decisions. Ego-driven leadership tends to produce chaotic environments where a lack of trust leads to speculative decisions.

In law enforcement, the action imperative is when pressure from superiors to "get things moving" is exerted upon the people charged to manage the event. As you will see, this imperative can lead to dangerous situations where we attempt to wrest control from the hostage-taker without building trust.

PRESSURE TO ACT

"We are going to do a hostage rescue."

These are arguably the most ominous words spoken during a hostage-taking event.

Hostages are most likely to incur serious injury or death during the initial "taking" and during a rescue attempt. In other words, the hostage casualty rates increase significantly when we go in to save them. It is a striking dichotomy.

On one particularly memorable hostage-taking event that lasted twenty hours, the ego and authority of our Incident Commander (IC) clouded his judgment, placing us on the precipice of doing something that would likely cause irreparable damage.

In violation of a court order, David Kelly, a forty-eight-year-old carpenter, had taken his nine-year-old son, Sean, from his estranged wife, Dot, at gunpoint the night before outside her place of employment.

Dot Kelly placed their son inside her vehicle as she saw David approaching. David expressed his intent to take the boy home. Dot refused to let the child go with him, at which point he returned to his car and retrieved a handgun.

Dot fled, and David drove off in her car with Sean.

Dot immediately called the police. Responding officers searched David's car, left near the location of the abduction, and found another pistol and a hatchet on the front passenger seat.

That evening, police obtained a warrant for his arrest, charging him with violation of the protective order. Officers went to the Kelly home and discovered Dot's car in the driveway. They attempted to make contact with David but got no response.

Shortly thereafter, Sean called his grandmother in Florida and told her, "My daddy has a gun, and he will shoot anyone who tries to take me away from him."

Multiple attempts to contact David proved fruitless. We spoke with him one time during the night. He said that everything Dot told us was a lie. He was with his son, in his house, and we would be better served leaving him alone.

As the sun came up, forward observers reported seeing the child clad in body armor inside the home. David was also seen propping a shoulder-fired weapon near the front door of the residence.

At about 6:30 a.m., we engaged Kelly in conversation for the first time since the "go away" exchange the night before. Although it was not the most productive of conversations, I viewed it as progress compared to nonexistent dialogue overnight.

Kelly called Sean's godmother. He told her he wanted her to come to the home at 8:00 a.m. and take Sean to school. We obviously were not going to let her do that. At 8:15 a.m., he called the godmother again. This time we sent a negotiator to sit with her on the call.

We had vetted the godmother as an appropriate third-party intermediary (TPI) and used her as our "bullhorn" to communicate with Kelly. The negotiator acted as her coach and was listening in on the conversation between Kelly and her.

When Kelly was told that police would not let the TPI approach the house, he referred to us as "pigs" and said, "Do not tell me I am going to have to kill a cop." Just before 8:30 a.m., another agency's HNT took over for my team. It was time for them to get some rest. I stuck around until about 10:00 a.m., when I, too, was ordered to leave.

I should have left when my team did, but my own ego and authority got in the way. I returned to the scene at about 3:00 p.m. As I exited my vehicle, I could tell the tenor of the event had changed.

It is difficult to describe, but you know how, in the summertime before a storm, you can actually smell rain in the air though it has not arrived yet? The leaves on the trees start to flip over as the wind increases. The sun is still out but is beating a hasty retreat behind sinister-looking clouds. It was that kind of feeling.

On my way to the command post (CP), I walked past the robot control stand. Two of my negotiators were viewing the video feed from the bot, which had been positioned just to the left of the armored personnel carrier (APC) parked in front of Kelly's house.

As I passed, I could see what had their attention. On the monitor there appeared to be a civilian, peeking around the back end of the APC, waving at the front of the home. This was wrong on many levels.

Why are we exposing a civilian to dangers we are not willing to expose our own personnel to? I thought as I continued to the CP.

I learned later that the other HNT was able to make sporadic contact with Kelly inside the residence by telephone while I was at home.

In these conversations, David sounded as if he was intoxicated. Negotiators speaking with him offered several opportunities to release his son and tried to convince him to surrender. Kelly stated that he would only release his son to the godmother or to his pastor if either came to his residence unescorted by police.

Again, this is not an option. The repeated pleadings with David to let his son leave were met with refusal. Throughout the day, Kelly repeated comments about how he might have to shoot a police officer to get what he wanted. He also confirmed that the shoulder-fired weapon observed by the sniper team earlier was indeed a shotgun.

About noon, David called his pastor (the civilian seen on the bot monitor) and asked him to come to his residence to talk to him. The team gave David the next best option and allowed him to continue talking with the pastor by phone, several times between noon and one o'clock.

During these conversations, David repeated his threats of shooting the police by asking if he would have to "start blowing pigs away" in order to prompt us into allowing a face-to-face conversation between him and the pastor. When the pastor informed Kelly that they would not let him approach the house out of concern for his safety, Kelly responded by saying, "If we cannot talk, we have a problem. It is a shoot 'em up problem is what it is. There is no choice."

A negotiator engaged David by phone until just before my arrival. Additionally, officers and the pastor in the APC attempted to speak with Kelly directly by using a public address system from the vehicle.

Kelly shouted at one negotiator that he was going to "put one between his eyes." Over the phone, he then threatened to shoot another negotiator because she "talked too much."

Mental health experts monitored the situation from the beginning. They concluded early on that Kelly was suicidal. They also noted that Sean was the center of David's life and he would not do anything to harm the boy unless someone tried to get in between the two.

It was also obvious David was drinking more alcohol as the day wore on. He occasionally ventured briefly onto his front porch to yell at the police. His gait and speech confirmed his alcohol consumption.

As I neared the CP, I could see my team supervisor, the one who had phoned me. This was odd. When I was not on-scene, she was supposed to be in the CP in my place. She was pacing back and forth outside of the bus.

It seemed that the senior executives saw fit to throw her off the bus.

Wait, what?

The senior executives' egos led to deviation from policy.

They surmised she would pose resistance that they did not want to deal with as they contemplated their next actions.

My team supervisor at the time was Amy (who Mike Falconer referred to in Chapter 4). Amy is strong-willed, opinionated, extremely smart, and a great leader. She called it as she saw it, and that ruffled feathers, especially of those birds who outranked her.

I had worked with Amy at various times during my career. She is a consummate professional who demonstrates great decision-making and always creates an outstanding working environment for those who work for her. To this day, she is the best supervisor I have ever worked with and for. I would run through a wall for her. Her judgment and situational awareness are exemplary.

Leaders like Amy challenge leaders who are bound to ego and authority; their fear of the Amys of the world gets in the way of sound, logical judgment.

Authors Jocko Willink and Leif Babin wrote, "Ego clouds and disrupts everything: the planning process, the ability to take good advice, and the ability to accept constructive criticism." This clouded vision was why Amy was not allowed to stay on the bus.

I opened the CP door. The chaos outside paled in comparison to what was going on inside. In my seat sat the commander of the other agency's HNT. He rose when he saw me, walked past me, and said, "This is fucked up."

I scanned the interior of the bus, which is not that big, and saw the chief of police, several other senior executives, the IC, and a host of others—far too many, according to protocol.

The Incident Command Triad, as the name implies, is supposed to be composed of three people: the IC, SOT (SWAT) Commander, and me. The SOT Commander and I served in a subordinate role to the IC, providing them with information from our respective teams so that they could make the appropriate decisions as to the resolution of the incident. The buck is supposed to stop with the IC. However, in this case, senior executives gave advice to IC in large part because they did not display much confidence in his ability to manage the incident.

They failed to empower him to make the right decisions. They second-guessed him, limited his responsibility, and micromanaged his tasks. They intentionally created a perception of autonomy while they maintained control over the incident. As observers of the IC, they directed him, primed him in how to act, and tried to dictate what he should do next. This is against policy, procedure, and practice.

In effect, they undermined his confidence, producing an environment in which he was reluctant to make a decision counter to what they were saying. I was floored and asked the IC what was going on.

"We are moving [a third agency's SWAT team] up to relieve SOT so they can get some rest. We are going to do a hostage rescue."

I asked what had changed in the time I was gone.

"He is suicidal."

I told him we knew that in the morning. I begged the question with more firmness this time. "What...changed?" I asked, pausing slightly between words for effect.

He added, "We are not sure how much longer the kid will go unharmed."

I reminded him what mental health had advised about David and Sean's relationship. I asked again, "What...changed?"

He said, "We are concerned about the long gun behind the door."

I told him we knew about the long gun earlier, asking again, "What...changed?"

He replied, "We are not gonna let this go into another night."

At that time, I had been a lieutenant for about a year. Because I was a new lieutenant and the IC was a captain, me saying a hostage rescue was not the appropriate course of action did not sit well with him. I could see it on his face. I could see it on the faces of the other executives who were assisting him.

Here again is the power and influence of ego and authority. Senior-level law enforcement officials have offline discussions with the IC during the management of a hostage-taking. They should not be directly involved in planning and implementation. This is the reason they select and train individuals who are subject matter experts.

Yet, their ego tells them, *You are an executive in this agency. You do not really have a responsibility here, but rather than just observing, go ahead and insert yourself into the process. That way you can validate yourself and your rank in front of your subordinates.*

To his credit, the chief did not say much out loud while he was in the CP, but his mere presence changed the environment and affected the decision-making. Ego hindered his ability to see that. Ego and authority promoted consensual decision-making during this event. While it was never spoken, the IC quietly ceded authority for the decisions to others, causing the situation to spin out of control with collective rationalization, lack of accountability, and pressure to acquiesce. In other words, groupthink.

They failed to analyze and fully appreciate the potential risks of a hostage rescue because they had their own ideas as to the outcome. They floated those ideas looking for support. If they got the support, it validated them. Once validated, the ego was triggered. In the Kelly situation, the decision-making power was diffused, which set the stage for problems to develop.

When there is a clear definition of who has what responsibility for decision-making, the chances of something going wrong are reduced, particularly if the person is knowledgeable and experienced.

The "action criteria" was developed by the CNU at the FBI for hostage-taking events, and requires that before taking any tactical action that will alter the dynamics of the event, the IC must be able to answer the following questions:

- Why is the contemplated action necessary?

  ○ What conditions changed to cause consideration of the action?

  ○ Why are we taking action now?

- Why is the contemplated action risk-effective?

  ○ Did we fully explore and attempt less-risky alternatives?

- Why is the contemplated action acceptable?

Clearly those who were running the show in my absence had not considered any of these questions or had chosen to ignore the conclusion. Here, ego and authority became impediments to making decisions in a highly stressed environment. Under the pressure of this event, risks were ignored because in their minds, consensus was better than conflict.

I reminded the IC that the two most critical times for a hostage are during the initial action and when we try to conduct a rescue. The SOT commander also voiced his concern about the proposed rescue. He agreed to call it off.

Remember, the action imperative takes hold when pressure from superiors to "get things moving" overwhelms proper management of the event. This is a dangerous proposition where we attempt to wrest control from the hostage-taker.

It usually ends in failure.

In this case, the emotions tied to ego and authority were so powerful that the IC and the rest of the decision-makers in the CP were seriously endangering life, merely to give David the impression that they were in control. But who was really in control? Think about it. If ego and authority are powerful enough to influence life-and-death decisions, how much more influence will they have on lower-stakes issues relating to the performance of your organization?

The IC whispered our veto to another executive in the CP. He then came back to me and said, "Well, we gotta do something to get a response out of him. Let's send the robot up the porch steps to 'break and rake' a window and see what kind of response we get."

I am not a tactical guy, but I do have some common sense. David was going to think it was an assault and kill either the kid and then himself or the bot. I shared my concern with the IC. His patience with me was starting to evaporate.

The SOT commander radioed his team as to what was being discussed. The response: "Hell no."

Their fear was if the bot became disabled, it would be another obstacle they would have to work around if an emergency action became necessary.

And...boom goes the dynamite.

In the course of five minutes, actions the IC wanted to undertake were shot down by his subordinate team members. So the IC was now caught in between us telling him no, no, no and the bosses telling him go, go, go.

While the IC agreed to call off the hostage rescue and the bot going up the steps, he was still suffering from the effects of the action imperative. Ego and authority would not allow him to let it go. He wanted to do something to show everyone he was capable and in charge. He wanted to show David. He wanted to show me. He wanted to show the SOT commander. Perhaps more importantly, he wanted to show the other executives that he was in control.

There was a lot of conversation between the current IC, his relief, and other executives in the CP. They plaintively asked if they could use the bot to take a bullhorn up to the steps of the front porch and drop it in an attempt to coax Kelly from the house.

Since I had moved them from the extreme position of hostage rescue, using a bullhorn as bait was not going to get much pushback from me. Nor did any come from SOT because they had already formalized the plan to take Kelly into custody once he came down the steps.

A look of satisfaction came over the executives' faces as they finally had an idea that was accepted.

Shortly before 4:30 p.m., the bot lumbered up the hill toward David's house with the bullhorn in its claw. It navigated the curb and dropped the bullhorn at the base of the stairs, and then it backed up about ten feet.

The plan called for one element of SOT operators to deploy to a position where they might be able to shoot Kelly with a Sage gun. This tool fires large, less-lethal, hard rubber projectiles in order to stun a person, hopefully knocking him to the ground to make apprehension easier. Coincident with the use of the Sage gun, other operators would deploy noise-flash diversionary devices, otherwise known as "flash bangs," designed to distract and disorient a person with a concussive explosion.

They hoped this would afford them an opportunity to rush David and subdue him without serious injury to him, Sean, or any of the officers.

The operators assigned to subdue David were prepared to use lethal force if his actions made that unavoidable. The plan also dictated that if they were able to lure David away from the house, under no circumstances would he be allowed to reenter the residence out of concern that he would harm his son or cause further confrontation.

David emerged from his residence and walked across the front porch. He sat down briefly on the top step leading to the sidewalk and then walked down the steps towards the bot. He was carrying a handgun in his right hand.

In a loud and commanding voice, the negotiator in the APC pleaded with David through a public address system to drop his weapon so as to warn other officers, who did not have the same vantage point. David disregarded these commands and descended the stairs. He picked up the bullhorn, which shattered in the street.

The sniper team radioed other members of the team who were concealed behind a vehicle parked in the driveway of the house next door and told them that David was armed with a handgun and had ventured far enough from the door of the residence that they could apprehend him.

At that time, the group of officers with the Sage gun began to move from behind the vehicle to the northwest corner of David's residence to shoot him with the less-lethal weapon. Simultaneously, the other group, consisting of five officers, moved from behind the other end vehicle and started toward David to subdue him once the Sage weapon had been utilized.

They were nearly twenty-five feet from where he was standing pointing his pistol at the bot. There was no intervening cover, and a magnolia tree partially obscured the view of the approaching officers.

As the second group of officers drew closer to Kelly, he continued to face the bot and seemed oblivious to their presence nearby. The first element reached the corner of the house and determined that they had no clear shot at Kelly with the Sage gun, as their vision was obscured by a trellis, railing, and assorted junk that Kelly had allowed to accumulate on the front porch.

Before they could adjust and acquire a new firing position, a member in the second group bumped the vehicle behind which they had been hiding and set off the alarm.

David turned toward the officers in the second group.

At this point, about fifteen feet or less separated them. A lead operator in this group shouted at David repeatedly to drop his weapon. He failed to comply. Facing the operators in the second group, he began to raise his right arm, holding the gun in his right hand. These actions were relayed back to the CP via the bot video feed.

Then shots were fired.

An operator in the second group discharged a three-round burst from his MP5, .40 caliber weapon at David. One round struck him in the jaw and exited the back of his neck, severely wounding him. The other two rounds missed. Almost simultaneously, two flash-bangs were thrown toward Kelly and exploded nearby in his yard.

In spite of his wound, Kelly turned and walked toward the steps to his house. But whatever occurred next, Kelly would not be permitted to reenter the home.

A second operator fired two more rounds at Kelly, striking him in the right side of his abdomen. He collapsed on the front porch. Other operators entered the rear of the house, where they found and rescued Sean unharmed.

Officers rushed onto the porch and summoned medics, who were staged nearby. David Kelly was transported to the hospital, where he was pronounced dead.

We normally hold debriefings after any hostage-taking event. The David Kelly debrief was heated, as I will explain further in the next chapter.

TAKEAWAYS

- Ego and authority produce emotions that negatively affect decision-making in life-and-death situations—and when the stakes are much, much lower too.

- Ego and authority can lead senior management to force their hand in operational situations, especially when they do not have confidence in their subordinates.

- Use the action criteria before taking an action that will change the situation. Simply ask yourself:

    ◦ Why is the contemplated action necessary?

    ◦ Why is the contemplated action risk-effective?

    ◦ Why is the contemplated action acceptable?

- Groupthink might be comfortable. But groupthink can get out of control and is difficult to predict due to a lack of accountability.

- Hasty action for the sake of action usually ends in failure.

CHAPTER 7

TOXIC LEADERSHIP

FOCUSING ON SHORT-TERM GAIN IS A RECIPE FOR TOXIC leadership, exacerbating insecurities, and breaking trust. In environments where toxic leaders are in control, their need for positive reinforcement, elevation of their status, and affirmation of their authority can have a devastating impact on people and organizations.

Hostage Negotiator Leadership is about building individual and organizational integrity, where leaders and employees trust each other to tell the truth.

Integrity is an essential leadership trait. Employees know that if their leader acts with integrity, they will treat them right and do what is best.

The most common lies told by leaders are those designed to save face. Once branded as untrustworthy, leaders have irreparably damaged their credibility.

Human nature causes us to view ourselves as honest people. As a result, we rationalize our behavior to align with that view, regardless of how it looks to an impartial observer.

HUMAN NATURE AND SELF-AWARENESS

"The brain is doing this constant dance of, 'How do I get more of what I want while holding onto the identity that I think I actually have,'" says Dr. Kevin Fleming, owner of Grey Matters International., a neuroscience-based executive development and coaching firm. "The brain is always wired to reduce dissonance."

We all have the tendency to rationalize lying. We adjust the story so that it lines up with who we think we are. That way we maintain our consistency. Human beings love to be viewed as consistent in thought, action, and word. If we believe we are fundamentally honest people, we rationalize our behavior to ourselves as ethical—regardless of how it looks to others.

Lieutenant Jeremy Patterson was given both clear instructions and latitude by the chief of police to revamp the narcotics section. Deputy Chief Thomas Riordan disagreed with the changes Patterson was making to the section—specifically, where the street-level narcotics unit would be housed.

Patterson was supported by both his captain and another senior executive. Each had their own internal conflicts with Riordan and their support of Patterson frustrated Riordan tremendously.

In the midst of all this top-level infighting, the sergeant for the street-level narcotics unit fielded complaints from his personnel about Patterson's changes and took them directly to Riordan. Riordan met with the entire unit.

During the meeting, Riordan informed them that he was going to be replacing the aforementioned senior executive and they need not worry about Patterson's plans because, "When I get there, things will change. You will not have to worry about Patterson. There will be shit on my dick or blood on my knife when I get finished with him."

An executive speaking to down-liners about their boss like that is the epitome of toxic leadership. It is destructive in nature. It is no wonder members of the unit felt they no longer needed Patterson to address their issues. They had a sympathetic and undermining ear of a senior executive.

In studying unsuccessful leaders, one of the things that they almost universally lack is either self-awareness (how they are being perceived by others) or empathy. The inability to view the situation through the eyes of another is virtually absent in their repertoire.

The negative impact of toxic leadership is ubiquitous. It matters not whether you are in retail, banking, coaching, healthcare, the military, or law enforcement. The antidote for me has been learning and using Tactical Empathy.

Toxic leaders who lack Tactical Empathy are more concerned with short-term gains and successes than they are long-term relationships.

Remember Colonel Reed from our focus on learning in leadership? He saw how the military was filled with people who were inclined toward action. When he decided to write about toxic leadership, he did so because he wanted to invest time, energy, and effort in providing leaders information that would help them improve. It kicked into high gear when he was appointed the directorship at the War College, where he was motivated to take an even closer look.

The more he looked, the more people reinforced his exploration of toxic leadership. Reed wanted to help these people suffering under abhorrent leadership. "Once I got into it, I could not let it go," he said.

Reed did not intend to become the father confessor for everybody in the army who had a bad boss. But that is exactly what happened. Hundreds and hundreds of emails hit his inbox, basically saying, "Let me tell you about the son of a bitch I work for."

One of the emails came from a lieutenant colonel who was commanding a reserve unit. He wrote about the toxicity of his brigade commander, recounting a training brief he delivered. At the conclusion of the brief, the brigade commander "ripped [his] face off."

Even though he had given the brigade commander exactly what he asked for, what he got in return was humiliation. He asked Reed what he should do. Reed advised him against direct confrontation because the brigade commander had significant power and could ruin his case as well as his reputation. The lieutenant colonel replied, "Well, I have already sent him the attached email," which basically said, "I am not gonna put up with this. You are not gonna treat me like this."

He had figuratively squared off with the brigade commander.

Reed winced. "Now it is you or him," he said. "Only one of you two can survive, and he has got all the cards."

Survival for the lieutenant, while not impossible, was improbable. As it turned out, the brigade commander's boss already had an inkling about his leadership. But to this point, he had never had enough current information to act on.

"I said, 'At this point you have got nothing to lose. Go to your boss's boss, and have a one-on-one with him and express your concerns.'" So he did. The boss initiated an administrative investigation and subsequently fired the brigade commander.

AVOIDANCE AND MISTAKES

Michael Ellison is the chief of police for a small municipal law enforcement agency. He has nearly four decades of experience in law enforcement, safety, and public policy. Prior to his current job, he rose through the ranks of a major law enforcement agency in another state, starting as a police officer in the late 1970s and culminating in his appointment as commissioner.

Ellison described being an "avoider" as being just as bad, calling it a cardinal sin in leadership. He is referring to those who avoid significant issues and decisions, which can have a paralyzing influence on moving the organization forward. The fear of making critical or difficult decisions is attached to their lack of self-awareness.

When put into a tactical context, for law enforcement, this may mean going into a building or conducting traffic stops. Law enforcement trains their people to be aware not only of themselves but also of the people with whom they are interacting and the environment. It is drilled into their heads so that it becomes second nature.

The same thing holds true for managers. Managers should be able to complete their tasks and survive their job—and "do it in a context where you have not only awareness of what is around you, but self-awareness in what you are doing."

What gets in the way? Sometimes managers are torn about who they are and how they are being perceived, which can lead to decision or action avoidance. The thinking is that if you do not make a decision, you do not make a mistake. If you do not make a mistake, it is harder to be judged.

Emotions are ever prevalent in workplace decision-making, actions, and significant conversations. Whether it is fear, anger, stress, or frustration, emotions are there. If you do not acknowledge that, you are already operating at a disadvantage.

Ellison has learned that as a leader, you have to be more responsive and understanding of your own emotional state at the time you make decisions or statements; however, his experience with the leave-seeking officer did not prevent him from other emotional missteps.

A number of times during his career, his visceral reaction directed his decision-making and conduct. He equated these reactions to those of a three-year-old child, but you do not have the luxury of behaving like a three-year-old when you are in charge.

Self-awareness means being prepared to bite your tongue.

JERK

For a time, Reed worked for Lieutenant Colonel Eric Ellman, whose conduct was driven by ego and authority.

His insecurities were so deep that he needed to constantly remind his people, "I am in charge here, and you are not. I am more important than you are."

He was not nurturing, and he was offended if one of his subordinates succeeded because he thought it took away recognition from him. He could not live vicariously through the accomplishments of others. Reed said, "That was the worst guy I ever worked for."

So Reed focused on shielding his lieutenants from Ellman's influence on them. Ellman was a toxic person. He was bitter and always looking for an opportunity to highlight his superiority.

At the time, Reed was a captain and company commander. Routinely, Ellman would show up in Reed's area and say, "Walk with me."

As they walked, he spotted a cigarette butt, a piece of paper, or some other discarded trash.

"Captain, what is that?" he asked.

Reed responded, "That, sir, is a cigarette butt."

Ellman replied, "I know what it is. What is it doing here?"

"Sir, it was cast here by a soldier who obviously had no pride in himself or his unit."

Ellman said, "Absolutely right, Captain, and that had better not happen again." Then he would storm back to his office like he was pissed off.

Reed went back to his office and made a mark on the calendar because "it meant that I was good for about another thirty days."

On another thirty-day cycle, Ellman walked up to Reed's predecessor and poked him in the chest with his finger. This was Ellman's way of drawing attention to the hole in the guy's T-shirt where the collar met the main fabric. Ellman put his finger in the hole, turned it up, and almost ripped the T-shirt off of him.

"Now, Captain, you are out of uniform. Go home and change, and report to me when you are in appropriate uniform," Ellman snarled.

Torn T-shirt guy was an Army Ranger—a hardened, trained killer. All in all, a pretty dangerous guy. Conservatively speaking, he probably ran through five to seven different scenarios in his head on how he could disfigure Ellman.

The Ranger shook with rage. Reed was certain the Ranger was going to play out one of the scenarios, but he did not. Discipline got the better of him. The Ranger maintained his composure, went home, changed, and returned.

Toxic leadership is a cancer within any organization.

INTEGRITY

The supreme quality for leadership is unquestionably integrity. Without it, no real success is possible, no matter whether it is on a section gang, a football field, in an army, or in an office.

—DWIGHT D. EISENHOWER

In many law enforcement agencies, major cases (usually homicides) are tracked on an acetate board. Those that are open are captured in red ink. Once those red cases have been closed, they are changed to black. During the murder investigation mentioned in Chapter 4, Carlos was inundated with tasks in order to change his murder from red to black.

He was under a microscope. The pressure to perform was intense. To further exacerbate his situation, he and the homicide supervisor, Rick, had a previous history that was less than friendly.

Rick was not mature enough as a leader to put their differences aside and separate Carlos from the tasks at hand. Instead of looking for ways to help Carlos succeed, Rick intentionally left him to struggle and put him in a position where failure was likely.

Ego and authority interfered with the conduct of the investigation.

Rick appeared more concerned with removing Carlos from the case than he was with changing it from red to black. Removing Carlos from the case would have given Rick personal satisfaction. Rick did not like Carlos. Never had. Likely never would. Mike Falconer could see the tension between the two, and it was building to an eventual out-of-control spiral.

The contention over the case came to a head, leading Carlos to demand a meeting with Rick. Carlos did not trust Rick. The mistrust was so deep that Carlos surreptitiously recorded the conversation between him and Rick.

"Hey, what is going on here?" Carlos asked, recorder running in his pocket. "I feel like you guys are shutting me out. Like you do not want me on this case. What is happening?"

Rick said, "You want off the case?"

Carlos replied, "No, I do not want off the case. I want to stay on the case."

Rick said, "You want off the case, you got it. You are off the case."

Carlos replied, "I wanna stay on this case. I do not want to be off it."

Rick said, "I do not care. You are off the case."

Rick immediately went to the investigations commander, Carolyn, and told her that Carlos had asked to be removed from the case and his wish was granted. Carolyn called Carlos into her office and asked him about it. Carlos told her in unequivocal terms that he did not want to be removed from the case. "That is a lie," is how he framed it.

Carolyn was confused.

Carlos produced the recorder, slammed it on her desk, and played the conversation he had had with Rick. The recording clearly illustrated that Rick had misrepresented the truth of the conversation.

Carolyn made the integrity issue worse when she said, "Okay, well, I guess you are back on the case. Now let's just leave this alone." She did nothing to address Rick's conduct.

Falconer said it was a disaster. He questioned (to himself) why Rick was allowed to remain supervisor for the case.

He thought that he wanted to quit. *I cannot do this anymore. I gotta go. It is terrible.*

Ego and authority were at the root of Rick's lie. He did it because he could. By virtue of his rank over Carlos, he presumed his word would not be questioned. He could not have gone into Carolyn's office and told her that he kicked Carlos off the case because he did not like him.

Rick was seduced by the opportunity that Carlos had presented him by asking for the closed-door meeting. Ego and authority clouded his judgment, causing him to act rashly and tell the lie. The closed-door meeting would also give him plausible deniability and allow him to save face.

THE EXPERTS

According to Tim Hird, Executive Director of Robert Half Management Resources (RHMR), "People want to work for those who are ethical. They know that if their leader acts with integrity, that leader will treat them right and do what is best for the business."

In a survey conducted by RHMR in 2016, both employees and C-suite executives rated integrity as the most essential leadership trait. However, a greater percentage of employees considered it the top quality in an executive.

David M. Long, a professor of organizational behavior, says, "Followers are willing to be vulnerable in a good way to leaders they trust and are more inclined to be satisfied with and committed to them."

With Tactical Empathy, we show our integrity on the hunt for rapport and trust-based influence. Trust is predicated on truth, and without trust, it is impossible for leadership to be effective. Many businesses and teams fail because leaders are ethically challenged. The reasons vary, but keeping within the context of this book, it has a lot to do with self-image and professional self-preservation. Both are inextricably tied to ego.

Looking back at the conclusion of the Kelly hostage-taking incident in the previous chapter, we held a debrief. This is a "hot wash" of the event that is attended by all of those who were involved, from the IC all the way down to the officers who were at the outer perimeter to keep the press and other looky-loos at bay.

I knew this debrief would be heated. Emotions were high because while David Kelly was responsible for his own actions, we did not want to kill him. But the actual shooting was not the core issue. It was the conduct of the senior executives leading up to the shooting.

The question we had to confront was how ego had influenced decision-making to such a degree that training, policy, and practice had gone out the window.

The mood was so intense that the debrief had to be terminated after a few heated exchanges that got us nowhere.

A few days later, word got back to me that during a meeting presumably with the chief, senior executives had said that I had not briefed anyone in the CP on Kelly's relationship with his son. They said if I had, no one would have contemplated a hostage rescue.

That was not true. But ego prevented them from admitting to their mistakes or telling the truth. This from people with and for whom I had worked for years. They knew what they did was wrong. But ego would not allow them to accept responsibility.

It was my fault, according to them. They made it clear that they were throwing me and my team under the bus. Leaders often resort to this strategy to save face. They succumb to perceived pressure from their bosses and followers. To them, there is little worse than being viewed as wrong or ill-informed—so much so that they are willing to roll the dice on degrading relationships and irreparably damaging their credibility.

The impact of lying for self-serving purposes is enormous. Biren Bandara, CEO and Founder of the Leader School Incorporated, says there are three common characteristics lying leaders often feel pressured into:

1. **It is not my fault the project failed. My team messed up.** The leader does not take responsibility for their actions. As a leader, your actions include those undertaken by your direct reports since, as the name implies, they act under your direction. Nothing kills credibility more than throwing people under the bus, especially people for whom you are responsible.

2. **Baffling them with bullshit.** This masks the fact that you do not know something with big words, hyperbole, and confusing statements. This is usually used subordinate to superior but is much worse coming top-down. It is completely transparent.

3. **Lying to yourself.** This is usually to minimize weakness or overestimating strengths. This may not always have the worst external consequences but can definitely have a major long-term impact. When you do not allow yourself to ask for help, it is self-applied pressure. Pressure creates stress, and stress makes you uncomfortable. Overestimating your capabilities and knowledge to feed your ego increases your chance of failure.

Bandara concludes by saying, "Lying to save face may sometimes seem like the only option when under the gun. It is not. Saving face is usually brought on by self-serving motives and generally results in a loss for someone else."

Adam Hanft is a brand strategist. He runs Hanft Projects, a New York City-based firm, and is a frequently published marketing authority. He sits on the board of Scotts Miracle-Gro and has consulted for companies that include Microsoft, McKinsey, Fidelity, and Match.com.

Hanft offers the following as explanations for this kind of deception:

INSECURITY

People lie when the truth is too painful or embarrassing or they perceive it as inadequate. Their self-perception is wildly different from the way they are viewed by others, and they harbor anxiety about being revealed. Outwardly they appear to embody success, but internally they question their self-worth.

New York-based psychoanalyst Elizabeth Singer supports this, saying, "Lying results from a deep-seated belief: I am horrible on the inside. I need to make up a bright, shiny self to show the world. If anyone ever finds out who I truly am, everything will come crashing down." Ironically, the lies they tell bring about the embarrassment they are trying to avoid.

SELF-DECEPTION

"People start saying something enough that they start believing it themselves," says David Reiss, a psychiatrist based in San Diego.

"Looking back on the history of these people, the pattern started before they were powerful. They got into the habit of inflating things out of lack of confidence," Reiss continues. "Once they got to a higher level, if they have gotten away with it, they think they will never get caught."

When executives reach the top levels of management, the seduction of the sycophants takes hold, and they start to believe their own accolades and lose sight of the truth.

"You have to be able to hold people accountable. What happens with leaders is there is nobody who is speaking truth to power," says David Gebler, President of Skout Group, which helps organizations manage people- and culture-based risks. "They have got themselves locked into a world where they really believe they are not doing anything wrong."

TAKEAWAYS

- Human nature causes us to view ourselves as honest people. As a result, we rationalize our behavior to align with that view, regardless of how it looks to an impartial observer.

- Destructive leaders are more concerned with short-term gains and successes than they are maintaining long-term relationships.

- Toxic leaders' insecurities are so deep that they need to constantly remind their people that they are in charge.

- Integrity is an essential leadership trait. Employees know that if their leader acts with integrity, they will treat them right and do what is best.

- The most common lies told by leaders are those designed to save face.

CHAPTER 8

EMOTIONAL CONTROL, DECISION-MAKING, AND MISTAKES

SELF-CONTROL IS AN ESSENTIAL COMPONENT OF HOSTAGE Negotiator Leadership. When we lose our self-control in a leadership setting, we risk losing respect from those around us. Because difficult conversations bring our emotions to the surface, we need to be mindful of the things that trigger us in negative ways, and we also need to be willing to own up to our mistakes. One of the biggest mistakes we can make is putting our own self-interest above the interests of our colleagues and employees in our decision-making and relationship management.

It has been said before that if you cannot control yourself, then you have no control over your future.

LOSS OF EMOTIONAL CONTROL

Back to the high-profile murder case.

Thomas Riordan, introduced in the last chapter, was informed by Rick that Mike Falconer was leaking information about the case to people outside of the agency, something Falconer had been questioned about in the past and vehemently denied.

While at lunch one day, Rick called him and asked what, if anything, he had shared with anyone about the case. Falconer was irritated and questioned the impetus of this latest accusation.

Rick became irate. "You are gonna tell me, and you are gonna tell me right now!"

This emotional outburst caught Falconer off guard. Proving that when attacked, our default is often to attack back, Falconer retaliated in his retort. He realized he should have just said, "Okay, fine. We will go over it again," but he was fed up. He told Rick he was at lunch and he would explain it *again* when he got back to the office, and then he hung up. What Falconer did not know at the time was that Rick had made the call from the office and in the presence of Riordan. Falconer called Carolyn and asked her why Rick was questioning him about the leak again. She told Falconer to report to Riordan's office immediately.

Falconer did as directed and was met by Riordan, Rick, and Carolyn. Riordan laid into Falconer.

"Why are you not telling my supervisor what he is asking you?"

Falconer explained that they had gone over the issue several times, and in his mind, it had been put to bed. Falconer put what happened next into psychological terms.

Riordan lost his shit. "I do not care! You never talk to my supervisors like that! You cannot do that shit! This is bullshit! You are not going to do it that way! Not with me! I want to know every little thing you told [the other agency]! You know, as a matter of fact..."

At this point Riordan stood up, pointed his finger in Falconer's face, and said, "I want you to write a statement! Everything that you guys have talked about in this case! Every little thing! You better do it right away! If you do not, there are gonna be consequences! There is gonna be hell to pay!"

Riordan stormed out of the office. Carolyn just sat there with an I-do-not-know-what-to-say look on her face. Falconer looked at Rick and thought, *I wanna punch you in the balls so bad right now.*

As you continue reading this chapter, reflect on the words that Riordan used: "telling my supervisors," "never talk to my supervisors," "not with me," "hell to pay."

How dare you? I am sorry.

When Chief Ellison was a sergeant, he had an officer who "frankly, got the better of me, and I lost control." When Ellison lost control, he lost the officer.

The officer requested leave that Ellison denied. So the officer did what many have done and still do. He went "supervisor shopping," meaning he went to find another sergeant to approve the request.

When the leave was denied again, the officer went to the lieutenant. Ellison just happened to be in an adjacent office when he overheard the conversation between the lieutenant and the officer. The officer told the lieutenant that Ellison was unreasonable.

Rather than walking in and repeating that the reason behind the denial was staffing, he took umbrage with the supervisor shopping and laid into the young officer.

Ellison could have very easily used it as a teachable moment, but he lost that opportunity when he lost control over his emotions. He blamed this on being a new sergeant. He thought, *Who is this officer who has the audacity to get a second opinion on my initial decision?*

Fortunately for Ellison, he had a mentor, a more senior supervisor, who reviewed the incident with him. Ellison recognized his mistake and went back with a little bit of honest humility and apologized to the officer for losing control, even though he knew it was likely too late.

"I screwed up big time, and I had to go and apologize. That was probably my first big mistake that I had to own up to."

Even when you own up to it, people may or may not accept it because they may not be confident that you truly understand what you did and how it was perceived. The damage that his ego and authority caused in that one moment took a while to repair.

GETTING TRIGGERED

Leading is a high-pressure job. Kyle Kensing, online content editor at CareerCast, says that the stress score for CEOs stands at 48.7, or almost ten times as high as the least stressful job in a study CareerCast.com posted in 2018. (For those who are curious, the least stressful job was diagnostic medical sonographer.)

Manage your triggers or they will manage you.

Because of the pressures associated with leadership, it is inevitable that something will occur that will trigger you. You have to have the wisdom to recognize it, pull it back, eat a little crow, and apologize when necessary. More often than not, an emotional decision will not be a good one because you are not thinking clearly.

Remember, when emotions are high, rational thinking is low. When we are emotional, whether we are in a difficult conversation with our spouse, kids, or whomever, we are not thinking rationally. Why would it be any different in a business environment for a leader? This highlights the advantage of time. If you have the luxury of time, walk away from the issue for a while. If a bad decision or statement leaves your mouth beforehand, have the courage to fall on your sword or reverse the decision.

In 2000, during the Democratic National Convention, Ellison was working on his agency's response to managing demonstrations that were occurring all over downtown. They did not have a chance to deliberate.

In some cases, they conducted planning exercises in anticipation of certain eventualities throughout the day. Accurate, measurable, and reliable information was available. But other times during the same event, they made a decision off the cuff. In this type of environment, the chance of bad decisions being made increases dramatically.

When this happens, how does a good leader respond?

Are you willing to stand up in front of everybody and say, "I made a mistake"? It is difficult for some people to do, regardless of whether they are a leader, manager, supervisor, mom, or dad because we are human. As such, we are reluctant to publicly admit our fallibility.

Most people want to see themselves in a positive light rather than having weakness exposed, so they are torn. Stress creates contradictory beliefs, opinions, and attitudes. As a leader, you want to think you are far too savvy to make mistakes. When presented with evidence to the contrary, stress can set in, leading you to deny your mistake or fail to apologize.

Admitting a mistake is not a sign of weakness. Admitting errors strengthens relationships with direct reports, colleagues, and bosses. It communicates in a powerful way that you are human, trustworthy, and relatable. Legendary Duke basketball coach Mike Krzyzewski (Coach K) wrote, "When a leader makes a mistake and doesn't admit it, he is seen as arrogant and untrustworthy. And 'untrustworthy' is the last thing a leader wants to be."

The greatest leaders in history are the leaders who can acknowledge their mistakes and learn from them. Today's leaders need to move outside their comfort zone and face the fact that being afraid of making mistakes or wrong decisions is the beginning of greater uncertainty down the line for their organizations and the people they serve. In other words, playing it safe today may result in a problem the organization cannot mitigate tomorrow.

When most think of toxic leaders, they think of the arrogant bully. But leaders can be toxic by being indecisive or doing nothing. Allowing bad things to happen is equally as toxic. Though some decisions may be the wrong decision, each one gets us all closer to understanding the right course of action.

When leaders play it too safe, they begin to lose credibility with direct reports and peers. Everyone wants to be the hero. No one wants to be the scapegoat, so no one wants to risk making the wrong decision. They surrender to fear and uncertainty, which promotes stagnation.

Self-preservation leads to what Ellison calls "turtle syndrome," where a manager who takes the first direct hit they have ever experienced in their career ends up figuratively or literally disengaging from the organization.

It is similar to turtles who get hit on the head with a raindrop: some retreat into their shells while others do not know what to do and flip over onto their backs. At some point, all leaders are influenced by the instinct of self-preservation. But hyperconcern about self-preservation is more reckless than building up the courage to weather a direct hit.

The key is to put the direct hit into perspective and into the context of the responsibilities of your assignment. If you are led to the decision because of the facts, you are doing the right thing. If ego gets in the way, you are not.

DO NOT RUFFLE FEATHERS

As a leader, you are more effective if you are both liked and respected. One without the other results in mission failure and damaged relationships. Strive to find a balance between the two as you create the character you want to exhibit as a leader.

Using Tactical Empathy, a good leader should meet with their key employees or managers frequently for one-on-one sessions to remind them of expectations and understand theirs. With a deferential delivery, you can help them grow and improve. When you create and deliver clarity of expectations and standards, there is less confusion and more effective delegation and accountability.

Holding people accountable can be confrontational at times. Holding people accountable involves difficult conversations. Many leaders avoid tension and conflict associated with progress discussions or performance reviews. Avoidance is detrimental to your organization and the development of your people.

Is it more important to be respected or liked?

Who said it has to be either-or?

Why ruffle feathers when you can build rapport without it?

IT IS A "WE" GAME

Leadership is a "we" game. It is not a "me" game. The best leaders keep their self-interest and the interests of their direct reports in mind. They are just as ambitious as the next person.

Personal interest and ambition are not bad things. The bad thing is when ambition gets in the way of taking care of their people.

Whenever it comes down to the employees' welfare and the narcissistic leaders' ambitions, their ambitions will win every time. The subordinates sense it. Most have a pretty good barometer on whether or not their leaders have their interests at heart. It is not hard to diagnose.

Deputy Chief Riordan approached Lieutenant Daniel Casey with his brow furrowed. He was clearly irritated. Apparently Riordan and another senior executive had entered a restaurant where Mary was eating with a colleague. The colleague spoke to Riordan and the other executive. Mary, a detective under Casey's command, did not.

Riordan wanted to know why.

"What is her problem?" *How dare she not acknowledge me?* was the buried question.

Casey was perplexed. How was Casey to know why Mary had not spoken to him? He had not seen her all day.

"Find out and get back to me."

"You want me to get her back in here, sit her down, and ask her why she did not speak to you?" Casey asked.

"That is exactly what I want, and I want the answer before she goes home."

Reluctantly, Casey told Mary's supervisor, Amy, to have Mary return to the office.

Mary arrived, and Casey asked, "Why did you not speak to Riordan when he came into the restaurant earlier?"

"Are you serious? You guys called me back in here for

that? That son of a bitch is such a baby. He is crying about a detective, someone four levels below him, not speaking to him? Unbelievable! After what he did to me and my family?"

Mary held Riordan responsible for the termination of her husband, also a police officer. Her betrayal, embarrassment, fear, anger, and frustration were understandable...at least to Casey.

They clearly were not to Riordan.

Casey reported back to Riordan that she was still smarting as a result of what had occurred.

"Fine. I am ordering you to send her to EAP."

EAP (employee assistance program) is billed as a voluntary work-based program that offers free and confidential assessments, short-term counseling, referrals, and follow-up services to employees who have personal or work-related problems. Supposedly EAP addresses mental and emotional well-being, but it is commonly viewed by those in law enforcement as a stigma.

Mary was furious.

Casey was dumbfounded.

Riordan was satisfied. He had imposed his will. One way or the other, she was going to acknowledge his station in life—ego and authority, along with their cousin, narcissism, at their worst.

Michael Lehr, President of Omega Z Advisors, says that people who fall into the trappings of power experience several changes.

The first is dopamine surges, causing increases in hubris and risk-taking. Dopamine is a neurotransmitter that helps control the brain's reward and pleasure centers. It also assists in regulating movement and emotional responses.

Hubris develops when self-confidence and pride reach extreme levels.

"When we behave in a narcissistic manner and see ourselves as superior with exaggerated self-belief and overwhelming contempt for others, we are following a hubristic path. Our overconfidence often leads to disaster, as we become incompetent due to arrogance and self-delusion."

Risk-taking, by definition, defies logic. Why do people gamble? Why do they BASE jump or swim with sharks? It is the dopamine. Those brief moments of ecstasy that keep most risk-takers coming back for more and more. Birth of an addiction.

Second, when people view themselves as more important than others, a sense of entitlement sets in. They assume they "deserve" a certain outcome—a promotion, a win, an accolade—because of who they are and their past efforts.

They think, *I earned it. I am owed. I am due. I know what I deserve.* Over time, this slowly dissolves the motivation and morale of the people around them. Their ego and authority will not allow them to value others' time, energy, and effort as highly as their own. It also causes them to overstate their abilities, render judgment, and create unreasonable expectations.

Third, rudeness increases as empathy decreases. Cruel remarks, condescension, and cutting people off or out of conversations is some people's modus operandi. Rather than subjecting themselves to it, the followers withdraw.

Deliberation decreases as well because while they are not always right, this type of leader is never in doubt.

"One of the most prevalent—and damaging—themes in our culture is the need to be right," wrote Mel Schwartz, a psychotherapist and marriage counselor. "From the more personal and mundane battle over who said what in the midst of an argument to the larger issues of politics, religion, abortion, healthcare, gun control, or climate change, being right is mandated. It quickens our pulse, causes us to shout, and can sever relationships. It is the raison d'être for most acts of hatred, violence, and warfare."

Lastly, support of "brown-nosers" or "yes men" is evident and sought. Narcissistic leaders want the rubber stamp of the people they lead. Followers often have real difficulty offering opinions because they lack the courage or the skill to approach this type of leader with a message that runs counter to what the boss is thinking, saying, or doing.

Sometimes they display excessive respect for the role of the leader, their station within the organization, or their responsibilities. Other times they view the leader as "nice," and people are reluctant to offer professional criticism to "nice" people.

The narcissistic leaders are well aware that they are not open to differing ideas. Dissension or disagreement has been met with negative consequences—transfers to difficult assignments, career paths impeded, and limited access to senior leadership.

Reed says the tendency for these leaders is to "one hundred percent eliminate those who showed resistance. This is a hallmark of poor leadership." They are incapable of receiving loyal dissent.

Before most major organizational failures, somebody raised a hand and said, "'Boss, this is not the right thing to do. You do not want to do this.'

"The response is to banish the dissenter to organizational Siberia. Permanent midnight shift watch commander or in the little office down between the elevator and the men's room in the basement.

"There is always a way that the organization can identify who is on the outs. They abjectly fire them or move them out of the organization."

This creates a culture of avoidance and reluctance among those who should be providing honest feedback. It leaves the leader ill-informed, isolated, and in trouble.

TAKEAWAYS

- If you lose your emotional control, you lose respect. If you do, own up to it and apologize.

- Emotions are always involved in decision-making. Keep that top of mind, and know your triggers.

- Avoiding decisions for the sake of self-preservation will ultimately kill your career. It is more counterproductive than making a mistake.

- Leaders who are committed to the status quo impede growth. They believe that holding people accountable rocks the boat, and they would rather not deal with it.

- People who fall into the trappings of ego and authority experience several changes:

    ◦ Dopamine surges cause increases in hubris and risk-taking.

    ◦ A sense of entitlement develops.

    ◦ Rudeness increases.

    ◦ Empathy and deliberation decrease.

    ◦ Seduction by sycophants is sought.

CHAPTER 9

BLUEFLAMERS

THE "BLUEFLAMER" RISES RAPIDLY WITHIN AN ORGANIZATION
and is rarely viewed as experienced or accomplished. To compensate for that perception, they are driven to micromanage.

The Blueflamer is in a new position that makes them uncomfortable. The aggressive management style is an initial response used to relieve the discomfort.

THE IMPACT AND CHARACTERISTICS OF THE BLUEFLAMER

- Micromanaging

- Arrogance

- Bullying

- Bad behavior modeling

Being a "Blueflamer" is not always bad, but people who are unqualified or simply not a good fit are often given leadership positions.

The best career-development path is to take on a variety of operational roles and become a student of the game before considering promotion.

The Blueflamer is a person who rises rapidly within an organization, spending the majority of their time at each level preparing to jump to the next. They are so named after the characteristics of rocket fuel after launch. The fuel burns blue-hot to provide for the rapid ascent as the vehicle is propelled into orbit.

Some people want the prestige that comes with a higher rank without working to obtain the necessary skills to succeed in that role. Their ambitions are high, and they are only focused on attaining the brass ring. Having spent little time at each level, the Blueflamers are rarely viewed as experienced or accomplished. They are viewed almost exclusively as people who provided enough correct answers during a promotional assessment or interview. Their people know it. They know it. They overcompensate for their lack of experience by micromanaging. They find themselves engaged in a constant internal battle to prove themselves, which translates into an overbearing management style.

The strange thing is that the Blueflamer is not necessarily doing it maliciously. They are doing it because they believe their image, reputation, and future elevation are hanging in the balance. This causes stress, and we have already discussed what that does to their ability to process and comfort level. As I mentioned previously, what we want more than anything else when we are uncomfortable is to get comfortable again as quickly as possible.

Often, people become micromanagers because they do not understand the duties of those under their charge and they fear exposure. Being a Blueflamer impedes the basics of delegation in that they want to make sure their command, control, and confidence are believable.

They wield control and power like a sword and morning star.

Ellison has observed this phenomenon both with Blueflamers and people who were promoted within a "normal" time frame. The bottom line is that their new position produces angst. Their aggressive management style is an initial attempt to achieve some relief.

Ultimately, most Blueflamers do not believe in themselves, and it is hard for employees to believe in leaders who do not believe in themselves. Followers do not need or even want perfect leaders. They want authenticity. Authenticity requires the Blueflamer to recognize that they are not bestowed with all the knowledge necessary to be successful in their current position.

BLUEFLAMERS LIGHT FIRES

The Impact and Characteristics of the Blueflamer

1. Micromanaging

How many employees have heard this? "I am not gonna get too deep into the weeds on how you run your shop. It is your shop. What I want is for you to make Marshall our next homicide detective."

This duplicitous statement is a perfect example of micromanaging.

The impact of micromanagement is often ignored. Everyone from the front-line employee to the C-suite recognizes when it occurs within their organization, but most fail to address it.

Executive-level personnel tend to overlook it either because it is never brought to their attention or it is what got them to where they are, and they do not see the problem.

Micromanagement undermines the autonomy of subordinates, with managers hovering over employees and monitoring everything they do. Micromanaging Blueflamers have no problem keeping employees after work, hounding them over the phone, or having them come in on their days off.

Blueflamers are reactive and prone to rush. Unintended consequences of hastily made decisions are given little consideration. Best-case scenario? Highly intelligent and motivated employees "leave" but do not leave. They disengage, opting instead to do nothing until instructed. They stop sharing ideas. They stop taking initiative. They stop investing in the organization and working hard because they know the Blueflamer is likely to change their work anyway.

Worst-case scenario? They actually leave.

2. Arrogance

A Blueflamer working the midnight shift calls the home of a crime analyst at 2:00 a.m. to get an explanation of the report she generated the previous day. The crime analyst is a nine-to-five employee. "I am up. She can be up," the Blueflamer says when asked about the logic behind the call.

There is a huge difference between leadership, confidence, and arrogance. Ironically, the Blueflamer's arrogance is compensation for insecurity. Making themselves look good takes precedent over leading their team. Blueflamers do not like sharing the spotlight and take recognition for someone else's ideas.

3. Bullying

Leading by fear and intimidation is a common coping mechanism for the Blueflamer They need to impose their will in order to offset the perceived lack of respect that they get from their employees. Their communication style is often aggressive and caustic, which gives rise to employees who hate coming to work, voicing an opinion, or otherwise contributing. If employees are only engaging in safe, noncontroversial activities, then the odds are good they are being led by the Blueflamer with relative impunity.

4. Bad Behavior Modeling

Employees learn about and adapt to the organizational environment from the moment they are hired. The Blueflamer's behavior runs the risk of establishing a workplace model that features self over organization.

If employees perceive that the characteristics of a Blueflamer lead to success, it is highly likely that some will look to emulate them, starting a vicious cycle:

- The Blueflamer gets promoted and takes over a new team.

- The new team initially starts to function better.

- The Blueflamer's lack of managerial and operational experience starts to manifest itself in how the team performs.

- Older, more experienced team members question what the Blueflamer is doing and where they are going.

- The Blueflamer starts to adopt the "because I said so" mentality.

- Older, more experienced team members withdraw and try to hold on until the next person comes in, or they transfer out or get promoted themselves.

- Younger, inexperienced team members see the success of the Blueflamer and try to emulate them.

- In two years, the Blueflamer gets promoted again and the cycle repeats, creating a future bad boss.

PROMOTING THE WRONG PEOPLE

Being a Blueflamer does not have to be a bad thing. Young, ambitious managers who work their tails off and aggressively seek to better themselves should be applauded. However, people who are unqualified or simply not a good fit are often given leadership positions, and it has a ripple effect throughout the organization.

Not everyone who is eligible for promotion is ready for promotion. Leadership requires a skillset that can be taught. People often evaluate the potential for promotion based on the employee's operational effectiveness in their current position. If they have demonstrated excellence, they are deemed capable of supervising others.

But they are being set up to fail. To avoid that, they will adopt the characteristics of a Blueflamer and struggle in their new position.

Ask yourself why the young or inexperienced employee is seeking a promotion. Is it because they have the talent and are ready to move up? Or are they just moving up the ladder by competing for an open slot? If they do not have the talent, experience, and industry knowledge to feel internally confident, how can they be expected to lead workers with years of experience?

Experienced employees taking direction from a new boss they view as incompetent can be disastrous. They tend to become impertinent and, consciously or subconsciously, undermine their new leader.

Just because a leader ascends rapidly does not mean they will not be an effective leader. But to be successful, you have to be humble and expand the breadth of your knowledge. Some leaders do not bother to look for that breadth of knowledge as they gain experience. They just focus on doing whatever will get them promoted.

To avoid these tendencies, leaders should build a culture where employees are encouraged to be on a career-development path that takes them on a variety of operational roles. Encourage them to become students of their profession, immersing themselves in the industry and creating a strong foundation to methodically build their careers.

TAKEAWAYS

The Blueflamer rises rapidly within an organization and is rarely viewed as experienced or accomplished. To compensate for that perception, they are driven to micromanage.

- The Blueflamer is in a new position that makes them uncomfortable. Their aggressive management style is an initial response used to relieve the discomfort.

- The impact and characteristics of the Blueflamer include:

  - Micromanaging

  - Arrogance

- ◦ Bullying

- ◦ Bad behavior modeling

- Being a Blueflamer is not always bad, but leadership positions are often given to people who are unqualified or simply not a good fit.

- The best career development path is to take on a variety of operational roles and become a student of the game before considering promotion.

PART III

HOSTAGE NEGOTIATOR LEADERSHIP IN ACTION

CHAPTER 10

THE QUICK TWO PLUS ONE

THROUGHOUT THIS BOOK YOU'VE SEEN THE GOOD, THE BAD, and the ugly of leadership. You can now see why Tactical Empathy is such an important leadership strategy. Now let's talk about how to employ it and how to execute.

Specifically, let's discuss how you do these four things:

1. Communicate.

2. Establish rapport.

3. Build trust-based influence.

4. Change your behavior.

The skills and strategies in the remaining chapters are predicated on understanding these four things in relationship to the human-nature response. The goal is to uncover hidden motivations in order to provide you, as a leader, the information you need to influence and create trustworthy relationships as well as maintain loyalty.

Much of what I will share probably runs against the grain of everything you have ever learned. In essence, it is like learning a new language. For those of you who are fluent in more than your native tongue, think back to how awkward and clumsy you felt when you first learned the new language. Think about how long it took you to become functional, let alone proficient.

The challenge with learning a new skill is never about its complexity. It is about its awkwardness. When your brain tells you that something is awkward, what it is really saying is that there are no cognitive maps or neural pathways yet developed for the skill.

THE QUICK TWO PLUS ONE

As I've shown, when we put expedience first, an opportunity for negotiation can quickly become a crisis. This happens when we put emotion ahead of logic, which eventually leads to our loss of freedom and autonomy.

Remember how a planned robbery interrupted a rapid response mission in Chapter 3? Mike and Steve's reaction to this turn of events was to do the most expeditious thing they could think of: take hostages.

Changing the "take hostage" mentality requires a change in attitude and behavior; we need a new language, new practices, and new neural pathways. Skills like *Labeling, Mirroring,* and *Silence* are all a part of developing the Tactical Empathy to handle difficult conversations. You do not have to be afraid of difficult conversations. Instead, you can look at difficult conversations as an opportunity to discover information and positively influence behavior.

With Mike and Steve, their thinking was constricted because of elevated emotions. This resulted in binding eight hostages with duct tape and laying them on the floor, with four in front of the front door and four in front of the back door, effectively making them human barricades in the event we tried to enter.

Once Dana got him on the phone, he allowed Mike to vent, dump his emotional bucket, and tell us his story. Mike had spent the previous seventeen years of his life in the penitentiary for armed robbery. Not jail. A state penitentiary. He was now thirty-four years old. So he was a juvenile when he went in the first time. While he was incarcerated, Mike was subjected to some of the most inhumane behavior you can imagine. He even developed a heroin addiction.

Mike said that he had not been able "to get it right." He told Dana that the "system" was not set up for a Black man to succeed in America today. Dana used what I call "The Quick Two" (Labels and Mirrors) and the "Plus One" (Silence). The more he followed that formula, the more Mike opened up.

Earlier that day Mike had gone to a Kaiser Permanente clinic in Washington, DC, to get a prescription for methadone to help with his addiction to heroin. He did not have the twenty-five-dollar copay and was denied service. Mike told us that his wife was all over him about getting a job, which he was finding exceedingly difficult, as it is with most convicted felons. He was starting to hang out with some of the same criminal elements that got him into trouble seventeen years ago.

He was at his wits' end, so he copped more heroin and slammed a needle into his arm. A few hours later, he drove to Alexandria to do what he thought he did best: rob a business.

Yet he failed at that too.

Mike then began to cry, at times uncontrollably. He gathered himself just enough to tell us that his name was not Mike. It was Keith. We knew he was Keith all along, but we were operating from his frame of reference, not our own. If he wanted to be Mike, we let him be Mike.

Admitting his real name was a watershed moment for us. It was the clearest indication of rapport up to that point. Likewise, even though he never mentioned Steve—and, in fact, denied that he had an accomplice—Dana never let on that we knew there were two bad guys inside. Slowly Mike's emotions began to dissipate. He was no longer yelling, screaming, or crying.

Dana had begun to return him to the NFL (normal functioning level).

Mike said he was tired of hurting people and it was going to stop right now. Keith then started releasing hostages—five of them. A nine-year-old boy, a nineteen-year-old pregnant woman, her twenty-one-year-old boyfriend, another woman in her early twenties, and Steve, posing as a hostage.

The dialogue continued, and by using Labels, Mirrors, and Dynamic Silence, Dana demonstrated Tactical Empathy that kept the conversation going.

Then Keith said it: "I gotta go, man." He was talking about suicide.

Dana begged and pleaded with Keith not to do it. Keith said it was his destiny.

Dana continued to beg. Keith ignored him. "I am gonna let them go, but I am gonna let you know right now, it is over for me," Keith said, speaking to both Dana and the hostages.

He continued, "Soon as I let them go, it is over. Everybody got that tape off. It is over. Everybody stand up. Everybody get to their feet. Is that your pocketbook, miss? Get your pocketbook. Grab your pocketbook. Okay, hold on for a second. Just stay there. What is your name, miss? Jill. It is okay. You got your pocketbook? Okay. Listen, Jill, when you get out there, I want you to look for my wife. She is a short, light-skinned, Black female. You cannot miss her. Her name is Cathy. Tell her that I love her and I am sorry. Will you do that for me?"

Dana thanked Keith for what he was doing, heaping praise on him in hopes that he would expedite the release of the remaining hostages.

"Oh yeah. I am gonna let them go 'cause it is over anyway. I am—I am done. As soon as Jill comes out, let the door close, and it will be over."

Jill came out. The glass door slowly closed, and true to his word, Keith shot himself in the head.

Would we have liked to have gotten Keith out as well? Of course, but Keith was the ultimate arbiter of his fate. Our job was to ensure those we were sent to protect went home. We accomplished that.

By using Labels, Mirrors, and Silence, Dana attacked the negative emotions motivating Keith's behavior and returned him to a more rational state, demonstrating that he understood the motivations behind Keith's behavior. Keith became more logical, ultimately determining that the hostages had nothing to do with his lot in life, which led to their release.

This was a classic hostage negotiation—a classic difficult conversation. And the skills worked.

LABELS

Labeling allows you to tentatively identify the dynamics, emotions, or circumstances implied by the other person's words, actions, or demeanor. This technique is an excellent way to begin and remains extremely effective throughout any difficult conversation.

Derived from *emotion labeling* in the ALS set, Labeling is one of the most powerful tools in your communication toolbox. At the Black Swan Group, we dropped *emotion* and just call it Labeling because it can be used for so much more than emotions. While emotions are important and you should never let one go by without hanging a Label on it, if you are saving your Labels just for emotions, you are missing other opportunities to demonstrate Tactical Empathy.

You can Label body language, facial expressions, or the environment. You can even Label cold, one-word answers and silence. When you say, "It looks like..." or "It seems like..." or "It sounds like..." and are met with a "no" or a "yeah" and nothing else, Label it.

Those one-word answers are likely to become a cascade of new information that you otherwise would never have gotten. We have found Labeling dynamics and circumstances to be as powerful in the business world as Labeling emotions.

Labeling shows that you are attempting to gain an understanding of the position the other person is in and the challenges they face. It assists in uncovering the factors that drive behavior. While business leaders have difficult conversations of all kinds with employees, probably one of the most difficult is dealing with a behavior issue.

As an example, Stephen is a ten-year employee of a large company with a worldwide presence. He worked his way up through the ranks, starting on the front line in a position interacting with the public. He was good at his job. He then moved to a technical position and traveled a territory first in a technical support role and then as a manager.

During his tenure, Stephen never had a bad performance review. He always exceeded expectations. Then a new boss came in, and for the first time in ten years, he received marks in a "needs improvement" category.

In his review, the boss noticed Stephen's eyebrows furrow, and he subtly shook his head from time to time. At one point Stephen openly stated that he thought he did much better and that he was insulted.

Instead of getting into an argument, his boss simply said, "It sounds like I offended you and you think you should be rated higher."

By using Labels, you are sometimes drawing attention to the obvious, but it does not matter. As I said, people love to have other people understand how they feel. That love outweighs any negative connotations they may have about you using an "obvious" Label.

By the same token, you should understand that any passion,

feeling, or expressed thought has both a presenting and a latent emotion. Labeling the presenting is good. Labeling the latent is better. There is simply more power in Labeling something that is *not* said.

Likewise, Labels help to determine likes and dislikes. A like is an expression of value, appreciation, or desire known as a positive. A dislike is a lack of appreciation, aversion, or reluctance to or for something—in other words, a negative.

The positive or negative emotions a person in a difficult conversation attaches to your words is a signal of their importance. Labeling shows that you are attempting to understand the impact your message is having on them.

By Labeling a positive, you reinforce it and encourage collaboration. By Labeling a negative, you dissolve it. Any negative they are feeling about you, the environment, or the circumstance is the filter through which they receive your message. With negative thoughts, the brain cannot perform at a high or even normal capacity. When a person is threatened, attacked, or afraid, it is difficult for them to take in and process new material, let alone think creatively or collaboratively.

When using this skill, you need to be careful not to deny the negative. Denying the negative puts the focus back on the messenger. A light shift in language can make a big difference. If someone is being a jerk, adding a "seems like" can help soften the blow.

Not every emotion has to be presented overtly or as a sharp dichotomy.

For example, people say that people who hate cheaters love fair play. Or people who are passionate about their significant other have little tolerance for those who are apathetic about their relationships.

These things may be trusted. But to defuse emotions, just make a slight adjustment: "It sounds like you do not like..." or "It seems like you hate..."

Labeling a positive is good; Labeling a negative is three times more effective. Think of them as two targets of equal size and equal distance from you. Shooting at the positive target gets you one point. Shooting at the negative target nets you three. Labeling a negative is three times more potent than Labeling a positive.

You can even *Mislabel* a dynamic to get to the core of a person's true motivation. Your employee's reaction to a Mislabel will reveal more information regarding what is important to them. You might say, "It seems like you are hesitant about these options." If the options are the issue, they will confirm it.

If the options are not the issue, you might get a clarification, such as, "I am not hesitant about the options. I am hesitant about the time needed to execute all of them."

Listening to what your coworkers and employees express by breaking down the components begins to slow time down without actually slowing the process down. Why? Because your brain is in high gear as you focus more of your faculties on communication and, consequently, slowly gain the upper hand.

As you prepare for your next difficult interaction with a direct report, write down a summary of the situation as you know it to that point. Then consider the predictable positive and negative issues or passions they are likely to bring up or be harboring when you get them into the office.

Prepare six Labels in advance (*Accusations Audits*. In Chapter 13, we will take a closer look at how to use Labels for Accusations Audits. To deal with them, Label early and often. Rule of thumb—every fourth vocalization should be a Label.)

MIRRORING

Part of the "art of listening" is making sure that the other person feels they are being listened to. One of the easiest ways to do this is to simply repeat the last one to five words or gist statements spoken by the employee. This could be something as simple as:

Leader: Would it be a bad idea if we talked about what is going on between you and Mark?

Employee: He is an arrogant a-hole who thinks he knows it all, and I am tired of dealing with his BS.

Leader: Dealing with his BS? Can you tell me more?

Mirroring can be especially useful in the early stages as you are getting acquainted with the employee in the context of a difficult conversation. It helps you gain initial information and begin building rapport.

Mirroring allows you to follow verbally wherever the other person leads, freeing you from the pressure of constantly directing the conversation. Under the stress of a difficult conversation, you may find you are unsure of how to respond to your employee. Mirroring enables you to be a full partner in the conversational dance without having to lead.

With Mirroring you avoid asking direct questions in order to gain information, which can sometimes put the employee on the defensive. You learn valuable information about the circumstances while at the same time providing the employee an opportunity to talk.

Leader: Dealing with his BS?

Inflecting upward on the Mirror says, "Can you tell me more?" or "Please go on."

Inflecting downward tells them, "I understand."

DYNAMIC SILENCE

Stop talking! Remember, it is not about you. It is about them.

Deliberately creating a void in the conversation takes the focus off of you. Dynamic Silence gives you the opportunity to present yourself as selfless. You are showing your employee that you are not concerned with trying to be heard and are more interested in learning. Rather than talking to show how smart you are or to reinforce the hierarchy, stay silent to show that you want to hear from them more than you need to be heard.

Dynamic Silence can be very powerful if used at the appropriate times. So when are the appropriate times?

Immediately after a Label or Mirror.

You will have the urge to justify your Label or Mirror by saying "but" or "because." We call it "stepping on" your Label or Mirror. Resist that urge. If you feel yourself wanting to say "but" or "because" after the Label or Mirror, replace it with Silence.

Another appropriate time to use Silence is before or after saying or hearing something meaningful. Silence encourages the other person to speak and, in the process, provide additional information. It helps to focus thought and interaction.

Silence is also an effective response to anger when the person you are talking with responds with a highly charged emotional outburst. When the outburst fails to elicit a verbal response, people often calm down. It is very hard to fight with someone who is not fighting back.

Even the most emotionally overwrought people will find it difficult to sustain a one-sided argument. Silence encourages them to return to more productive dialogue, no matter how uncomfortable it is for you. It is equally uncomfortable for the other person. By remaining silent at the right times, we can actually move the conversation forward.

When you are exposed to a new skill, you have to make new connections between neurons in your brain to manage it. In terms of understanding Tactical Empathy and the human-nature response, your visual cortex interprets body language and other unspoken affective cues. Your auditory cortex processes the hidden motivations contained in a spoken response, and other regions of the cortex compare and contrast the input with existing knowledge.

Dr. R. Nathan Spreng, a neuroscientist at Cornell University in Ithaca, New York, has studied how the brain morphs as we learn. Evaluating frontal magnetic resonance imaging (fMRI) and positron emission tomography (PET) scans, he found that we become more attentive when we learn a new skill. But the areas of the brain sparked by learning become less active over time if we do not provide new stimulus.

Meanwhile, areas of the brain associated with daydreaming become more active as people become more familiar with a task. The more you practice, the less you have to think about what you are doing. How long will it take you to develop a new skill? Studies show about sixty-seven repetitions. It is all about repetition, repetition, repetition. The more you do it, the more confident you become.

The awkwardness you experience developing these skills can be a powerful motivator for you to stop using them. I urge you to resist. Awkwardness is the key to accelerated learning.

Embrace it.

TAKEAWAYS

- Learning the skills of Tactical Empathy is like learning a new language.

- The Quick Two, Plus One showed you how to put those skills into practice.

- Labeling is tentatively identifying the dynamics, emotions, or circumstances implied by the other person's words, actions, or demeanor. "It looks like," "It seems like," or "It sounds like."

- Mirroring allows you to follow wherever the other person leads the conversation and demonstrate that you are listening by repeating back the last one to five words or the gist of what they are saying.

- Silence gives you the opportunity to present yourself as selfless. With it you show you are less concerned about yourself and more interested in learning about them.

- Look at a difficult conversation not as an opportunity to impose your will but as an opportunity to discover information. With a discovery approach, you can gain information that will help you influence behavior.

CHAPTER 11

DELIVERY, CALIBRATED QUESTIONS, AND PARAPHRASING

PERSON-TO-PERSON COMMUNICATION IS COMPOSED OF THREE features: content (the literal meaning of the words), tone of voice (including inflection, cadence, etc.), and body language (how the person stands, facial expressions, how they place their hands, arms, and legs, etc.).

When I think of these core features, I am often reminded of the famous line from the movie *Cool Hand Luke*: "What we've got here is failure to communicate."

How many times can we say the same thing about everyday circumstances or the difficult conversations we have in our personal and professional relationships? "Communicate better" is always good advice, but a few variables make it difficult, like different personality types, skills, and communication methods.

Regardless of the technique you use, how you say something is always more important than what you say.

Now that you have been given the Quick Two Plus One, let's talk about *Delivery, Calibrated Questions,* and *Paraphrasing.*

DELIVERY

UCLA Professor Albert Mehrabian (a communications studies pioneer since the 1960s), whose research provided the basis for the widely quoted explanation for the effectiveness of spoken communication, argued that:

- Seven percent of meaning is in the words that are spoken.

- Thirty-eight percent of meaning is paralinguistic (the way that the words are said).

- Fifty-five percent of meaning is in facial expression.

Mehrabian did not intend for this model to put an end to exploration on the subject, but it is pretty insightful. So much so that we use it at Black Swan Group because we see firsthand how important it is to understand how our communication affects human-nature response. Paying attention to the tone of your voice and body language is as important as paying attention to the tone of voice and body language of the person you are in conversation with.

How tone of voice and body language align with the literal meaning of the words is critical to understanding the totality of the message. You can take the sentence "I could just kill you!" and change its meaning entirely based on which words you emphasize, your inflection, and your tone of voice.

Again, this is a two-way street. The person you are communicating with will interpret this in much the same way, whether consciously or unconsciously.

One way to improve your interpretation skills is to Label tone of voice and body language. When someone says *yes* but hesitates, you can say, "I heard you say yes, but it seemed like there was some hesitation in your voice," or "I heard you say yes, but it seems like something I said concerns you."

Speaking with an *Assertive* (more aggressive), *Analytic* (colder and dispassionate), or *Accommodating* (playful, funny, and upbeat) voice will have a major impact on how a message is delivered or received.

When I use an Assertive voice, people are more likely to respond with poor judgment when they are under stress.

When I use my Analyst voice, most fail to really take notice.

When I use my Accommodator voice, a transformation takes place to a more cognitively nimble conversation in a positive frame of mind.

Shawn Achor, one of the world's leading experts on the connection between happiness and success, said in a *Forbes* article, "Every single business and educational outcome improves when we start in the positive rather than waiting for a future success. Sales improve 37 percent cross-industry and productivity by 31 percent. You're 40 percent more likely to receive a promotion and nearly ten times more engaged at work, live longer, get better grades, your symptoms are less acute, and much more."

In addition, people are six times more likely to agree with someone they like. So it is good to stay away from harsh, sarcastic, or punishing behavior. Smiling at appropriate times during the interaction enhances the person's positive state.

The 7:38:55 ratio can be used as a guideline to line up what someone says with how they say it. When someone's tone of voice or body language is not congruent with the words they say, use Labels to uncover what lies beneath. You should also use Labels to stay aware of your own delivery to keep it where it should be.

POOR DELIVERY OF BAD NEWS

For a good example of how this can play out, let's go back to Colonel Reed, who I highlighted earlier in the book. Reed worked for a boss he really liked, despite the fact that "he was an ass-chewing artist. He could bring a young soldier in and reduce him to a quivering pile of jelly in no time at all. I mean, I was in awe of this."

He tried to teach Reed his technique, but Reed could not do it. It just was not him. He would try it, but it never felt right. On one occasion, Reed was dealing with a problem soldier. The soldier was oppositional, defiant, in trouble all the time, and unrepentant.

They tried everything but could not make an impact on him. The decision was made to "chapter" him out of the army for unsuitability, which is when you discharge a soldier for performance issues that are irrevocable.

Reed called him into his office and said, "This is the last conversation we are ever gonna have on active duty." He wanted to yell and scream because of the trouble the soldier caused, but he did not. He talked about the nobility of what they were trying to accomplish and how bad he felt because the soldier was not going to be a part of it.

He also told the soldier he was disappointed because he and his noncommissioned officers had failed him. He then told him that "this was the end of the road." There was nothing that could be done. He was going to leave Reed's office, get on a bus, and go on to his next life. It was that simple.

The soldier started to tear up.

This was the first emotion Reed had ever seen from this guy. The only thing he had seen from him up to this point was recalcitrance. A tear dropped onto his cheek. "I said to myself, *Oh my God. I am finally getting through.* All this time, I have been unable to reach this young man, and now we are having a breakthrough here."

Before long he was sobbing. Reed got up, shook his hand, and wished him well. Reed opened the door, and as the soldier walked out, he walked past the master ass-chewer. "My boss looked at him and let him pass, and then he walked into my office and said, 'That's how you chew an ass.'"

WHEN CIRCUMSTANCES CHANGE

Communication styles change based on the circumstances. The appropriate communication style for when the enemy is inside the wire and you are passing out the last rounds of ammunition is different than the appropriate style for when you are addressing a team of individuals about a proposed change in the market approach.

With the former, the approach should be authoritative and direct for a very short period of time. With the latter, the best approach would be to slow down and attempt to understand the negative opinions, assumptions, and impressions the team will have with the new market strategy.

Effective leadership is when you meet the needs of the followers and the demands of the situation. Bad leadership—toxic leadership—is when the message is inappropriate either for the followers or the demands of the situation.

Delivering the news to your employees who do not want to hear it is tough. It is even harder when you do not agree with the message or decision you are communicating. Maybe you have to tell your star performer that they are being passed over for promotion, or you are informing your team that they will no longer be assigned take-home cars or telecommuting is no longer an option. In preparing for the conversation, draft a list of *Accusations Audits* (Chapter 12) to address the negatives likely harbored by the recipients of the message. These are preemptive Labels used to dissolve the negatives. You are, in effect, taking permission away from the other side from using those negatives against you in a difficult conversation.

CALIBRATED QUESTIONS

Calibrated Questions (CQs) are similar to open-ended questions.

These questions begin with who, what, when, where, why, and how. Open-ended questions (OEQs) exclude verb-led questions. Questions that begin with can, will, is, are, do, does, etc., can be answered with a yes or a no or closed-ended questions (CEQs) provide little information.

CQs tend to elicit longer responses and more information. The difference between a CQ and the traditional OEQ is with the CQ, we drop the who, what, when, and where because those sorts of questions can be answered too succinctly.

Nearly any CEQ, with some effort, can be reworded into a CQ. "Does that sound like the right move?" can become "How does that move sound to you?" or "What about this move works for you?" You can even ask, "What about this does not work for you?" Any will likely trigger useful information.

Well-timed CQs cause people to stop and think.

Aggressive conflict management types love CQs because they give them a feeling of control. The secret to gaining the upper hand in a difficult conversation with a control-oriented person is giving them the illusion of control. CQs are very effective in accomplishing this.

Very cautious, analytical types will often want time to think before they respond. CQs work with them as well, but the reaction is often delayed.

CQs are basically what and how questions. They should be asked early and often.

CQs are extremely valuable when you are faced with:

- A proposed direction change for the team or organization: "What are we trying to accomplish?"

- Notifying a subordinate about an unanticipated transfer to a new job: "How is this going to impact your home life?"

- Ambivalence or confusion about a problem: "What is the core issue here?"

- The viability of a proposal: "How is that worthwhile?"

- Determining how you can help: "What is the biggest challenge you face?"

- Clarifying an idea: "How does this fit into the objective?"

- Uncertainty: "What are we up against here?"

- Implementation: "What gets in the way of _____?" "How will you do that?" "How does that affect things?"

- An impasse: "What happens if we fail?"

- And my favorite, used to elicit exactly what it will take to move the needle with the other person: "What has to be true in order for _____?"

Your go-to CQs are "What makes you ask?" or "What makes you say that?" People do not ask great questions or they make statements that cloak an ulterior motive. These two CQs are designed to ferret out the hidden message in the questions or statements during difficult conversations.

They should be locked and loaded and ready to deploy at any time.

Notice I am not suggesting you ask, "Why do you ask?" or "Why did you say that?" There is a real distinction.

Universally, "why" makes people defensive. I have had the opportunity to train businesspeople around the world in hostage negotiation principles and have seen "why" set people off everywhere. For whatever reason, across cultures, races, and genders, it has become part of human behavior to ask someone why when we think they are wrong.

As an experiment, at your next opportunity ask your boss why they want something. Next, ask a peer a why question, and then ask someone younger than you or a subordinate a why question.

The reactions will include some level of defensiveness across the spectrum. Why? First, it sounds accusatory.

Second, it implies there is a right answer and they do not have it. "Why" is often well-intentioned. When we throw out a why, we are not trying to agitate people, but, on some level, that is exactly what we do. Its effect is undeniable.

Of course, the problem is that as the boss, quite often you really need to know why. So here is how to finesse why. Substitute "what."

"What made that a good choice?" "What made you want that?" Even "What caused you to do that?" is much more likely to get a good answer than "Why did you do that?" What is always the better alternative to why and a much more effective way to get information. Once you get the response, prepare to Label or Mirror it.

Does that mean you should never ask why? No. Here is how you can (in a very *calibrated* way) use it effectively when we want someone to defend a position that benefits us. This is the defensiveness you want to provoke.

"Why would you want to come to our team/me?"

"Why would you change from the way you are doing things now?"

"Why did you agree to take this meeting/call?"

When you ask this type of why question as a leader, they will not respond with, "Because you are a liar. You are incompetent. You treat people unfairly. You are the consummate micromanager." Instead, they will list all of the characteristics that you or the situation possesses that make their decision a good one. This is important, especially when you are trying to influence them to support or buy into change or an idea. It is harder for them to balk at your ask when they have already told you how great you are.

They articulate your value proposition before you ever have to say it yourself.

We frequently ask this question of new training or coaching clients. "Why do you want to take business negotiations training from former hostage negotiators?" The respondent then proceeds to tell us all of the value they see in our providing their training.

PARAPHRASING

Paraphrasing is a negotiation skill that focuses on content. The definition of this skill is very close to what is found in any dictionary. With Paraphrasing, you are listening to the literal meaning of what is being said and using alternative words to repeat it back to convey the same meaning. Paraphrasing demonstrates an attempt to understand the facts *and* the feelings. So it is different than Mirroring because you are *not* repeating back to them exactly what they have just said.

Paraphrasing can also be used when a longer message is being relayed. It should be used in relatively short bursts rather than waiting until the end of the long message. To do this effectively, you may need to check in and occasionally interrupt the other person to demonstrate the meaning of what you are hearing.

Some people may find this disconcerting because they have been conditioned to view an interruption as a takeover of the conversation that takes away their permission to speak. Prior to beginning the dialogue, it is useful to advise them that you would like to Paraphrase them while they are speaking just to make sure you are getting it right.

I tell them that as soon as I finish Paraphrasing, I'm going to give the conversation right back to them. Once they are prepared for and then get used to it, they are surprised at how much they like being listened to this well.

Here's how CQs and Paraphrasing (along with Labels and Mirrors from the previous chapter) look and sound like in a difficult conversation.

The employee, Judy, works for a large retailer and is transferred from one position to another, an important HR role. Internal complaints soon follow, which set the stage for an unpleasant midyear performance review.

Leader: What is your future plan? (CQ)

Judy: I am not sure what you are asking.

Leader: Not sure? (Mirror)

Judy: No.

Leader: It seems like I was unclear. What would you like to achieve in this job? (Label, CQ)

Judy: Why are you asking me this? I love this job. (She bursts into tears.)

Leader: (Hands her some tissue and continues.) I am sorry. It looks like I said something to upset you. That was not my intent. What is causing that? (Tactical Empathy, Label, CQ)

Judy: You guys threw me into this position. You gave me no training. I do not have any experience. I have no idea what I am doing!

Leader: It seems like we put you into an untenable position, and it sounds like you are frustrated with the job and with us because we threw you in the deep end. (Label, Paraphrase)

Judy: (Still crying.) Yes! I am dedicated and want to do a good job, but you guys have left me hanging. Now no one has confidence in me. Everything I have done is wrong.

Leader: (Silence)

Judy: I am just rudderless right now. The pressure has been a lot. People are complaining. It is awful. If I had a little time and a little guidance...

Leader: So it sounds like you feel like we abandoned you and left you to your own devices. And it sounds like if you had been given some coaching and instruction, it would have made your transition easier. (Label, Paraphrase)

Judy: That is right. You guys just threw me in there hoping I would figure things out and get on track. Well, I am not superhuman.

Leader: I am very sorry, Judy. It seems like we let you down. (Label)

Judy: (Nods.)

Leader: What would have to be true for you to say, "I am happy in my current position, and I feel like management has put me in the best position possible to be successful?" (CQ)

With that, Judy laid out exactly what she would need to do her job better.

TAKEAWAYS

- The Mehrabian ratio of 7:38:55 can be a helpful tool. It reminds us that communication comes in many forms: literal meaning, tone, and body language.

- A positive tone puts the other person in a positive frame of mind so you can collaborate.

- Calibrated Questions (CQs) are great for generating robust responses. Nearly any closed-ended question can be changed to a what/how question.

- Paraphrasing is listening to the literal meaning of what is being said and putting that meaning into another form.

CHAPTER 12

ACCUSATIONS AUDITS AND NEGOTIATOR PERSONALITY TYPES

TACTICAL EMPATHY SETS A COURSE THAT ATTACKS negative emotions, impressions, assumptions, or opinions by demonstrating that you are trying to view things from the other person's frame of reference. Because our attitudes are naturally influenced by negative emotions, learning a new language and behavior pattern that resets difficult conversations in a positive light is so important.

The *Accusations Audit* is another tool to create the right framework, ask the right questions, and use the right conversational posture in the right situation.

ACCUSATIONS AUDIT

How do differences inform our conversations? What negatives does the other side harbor that we want to deny, minimize, or eliminate?

Motivational speaker Tony Robbins says, "To effectively communicate, we must realize that we are all different in the way we perceive the world and use this understanding as a guide to our communication with others."

Tactical Empathy begins with the Accusations Audit (AA) to attack your counterpart's negative emotion, impression, assumption, or opinion. As long as those negatives go unaddressed assess differences and guide our communications away from the negativity that can cloud our handling of difficult conversations.

How do you deliver AAs? This is a recommended blueprint. You are the ultimate arbiter as to what you actually say during your difficult conversations. That said, when considering AAs, go all in—meaning if you have ten, use all ten.

Here is the general outline of your difficult conversation.

Summary: Summarize the relationship from the beginning up to the current point in time. This could be something like, "Thank you for taking the time to attend this meeting. We have been working together for X, and you guys know you are very important to me and the overall mission of _____. We have been through Y. We have weathered a lot of successes and a few failures. All in all, you are some of the best that I have worked with."

AA: Get out in front of the reaction.

- "You probably think that we are disorganized and we do not have a clear idea of the direction we want to go in."

- "You may be thinking that this is punitive in some way."

- "You might think that we are trying to make our jobs easier by making yours harder."

Why? Ask a why question, if applicable, to get them to support your position.

- "Why do you want to work for our agency?"

- "Why would you ever consider joining my team?"

AA: Hit them with one or two more right before you get to your ask idea, core idea, or bad news. At the very least you should throw out, "This is going to sound horrible."

Case in chief: This is where you make your ask, state your objective, or resolve the issue.

The following example does not involve a superior–subordinate relationship, but you will be able to imagine a similar circumstance in your environment.

MAKING THE ASK

In September 2016, a fellow negotiator at the FBI and I were having a conversation in which he was relaying his experience at a two-week hostage negotiation school he attended in Spain. There he met Claudette, a negotiator from France's primary national counterterrorism force, Recherche,

Assistance, Intervention, Dissuasion (RAID). RAID's practices in hostage negotiation have a lot in common with the Bureau's Hostage Rescue Team (HRT).

Claudette had been involved in two major terrorist events, one in 2015 at the Bataclan Theater in Paris and the other in 2016 in the town of Magnanville, about thirty-four miles west of Paris. Tate, my FBI friend, said it would be valuable if we could find a way to get Claudette to the United States to share her experiences with US negotiators.

I agreed and asked how he was going to do it. He worried that routing a request like this through the Bureau would be the equivalent of trying to run through mud eighteen inches deep. He thought it would be easier to go through the Washington Metropolitan Area Council of Governments (COG). Turned out, it was not.

At the time I was the vice chair of the newly formed negotiator's subcommittee at COG that had yet to establish a training fund. The cost to get Claudette to the United States for three days was estimated to be in the neighborhood of $10,000. A representative at COG told me that the more tenured SWAT subcommittee was sitting on close to $80,000 in unspent training funds that had been available for nearly three years.

He gave me the contact information for the SWAT subcommittee chair, and I reached out. Irwin, the chair and a state trooper for the Virginia State Police, agreed that it sounded like a great idea but said that he could not make a decision of this magnitude unilaterally. I would have to address the entire group of SWAT operators who represented the twenty-four member agencies of COG. He put me on the agenda to speak at their next meeting.

So far, so good.

The relationship between SWAT operators and negotiators historically has not been warm and fuzzy. There was a time when you could ask a SWAT operator what their impression of a negotiator was, and they would reply with names like a mouth marine, tree hugger, or give-peace-a-chance nut. "All they want to do is talk about feelings."

If you were to ask a negotiator the same question about SWAT guys, you would hear things like Velcro-wearing, tobacco-dipping door kickers. "All they want to do is shoot people and break things."

Most people would say that each team's mission, when it comes to hostage-barricade management, is diametrically opposed to the other's. This misconception was prevalent for many years. Thankfully, some of those misconceptions have changed. But there is still an "us versus them" specter in the air.

Prior to the meeting I prepared a list of AAs:

- "Some of you do not hold negotiators in the highest regard."

- "You guys think of me as an interloper."

- "You probably think I am here for an unwarranted money grab."

- "You are probably questioning my audacity at coming in here to ask for something that I had no part in generating."

- "You may question the value of this type of training."

- "Some of you may take offense at my being here."

- "You may even think I am just being greedy."

- "My being here is probably a complete waste of your time."

These are the negative opinions, assumptions, and impressions I thought they might convey in response to me and my message.

The day came, and I showed up at the appointed time. As I approached the doorway to the conference room, I could hear the banter. When I entered the room, the banter reduced significantly. All eyes were on me. I took a cold read of the room, scanning to see if my AAs were on point.

I noticed a guy staring at me while leaning back in his chair. His facing said, "Why are you even here?" I saw two other guys sitting together. One leaned toward the other and whispered something. They both then looked at me and smirked.

My AAs were right on point.

The meeting was called to order. I listened to some of the old business, and then it was on to the new. I was at the top of the list. I stated all of my AAs and followed them with a summary of why I was there. One guy in the audience spoke: "I, like everyone in this room, like case studies, but if we were to vote for this, it would set a precedent."

"Precedent?" I Mirrored.

"Yeah. We usually use that training money for more tangible things like explosives and sniper training. We do not use it to fly people in to talk."

"Sounds like you are questioning the value of this case study." Here, I used a Label.

"No, no, no. It sounds interesting, but I, for one, am worried that if we approve this, we are obligating ourselves to do it for other subcommittees, like K-9."

I told them I could not speculate on what the K-9 subcommittee would do but assured them this was a one-time ask for us. Our intention was to begin soliciting the chief of police group for a training fund similar to what they had in place, but arranging that for this venture would take more time than we had.

I concluded my presentation and thanked them for the opportunity. Two days later, Irwin emailed me and said the group had approved our request for $10,000.

Whenever you are going to engage anyone in a difficult conversation, the AA shows that you are attempting to appreciate their point of view. It is worth repeating: the AA reduces the chance of using negatives against you. It allows them to focus on your message rather than the negative reaction that might be going on internally, which will expedite your ability to build rapport.

If you do not address the negatives before getting to your objective, the negativity will be bouncing around their heads because of the brain's natural reactive biases. While our negative biases help keep us alive by helping us avoid danger, they can also keep us from making progress in key life moments and relationships. AAs are designed to eliminate the negatives and help set the framework for moving the conversation forward. As highlighted in the SWAT committee example, using AAs at the beginning of your difficult conversation will pave the way for a better outcome.

Do not be afraid to skip the pleasantries and small talk and jump right into an AA to attack the negatives. These negatives are the product of fear. As long as there is a remote feeling of fear or that you are a threat, dialogue is less likely to take place and lead in a positive direction.

You are a smart person. You know your employees and coworkers well enough that you can probably predict the emotion or response you are likely to receive. It gives you a tremendous advantage when you address the negatives before you get into presenting your case.

ASSERTIVES, ACCOMMODATORS, ANALYSTS

Most of us view ourselves as cerebral, logical, and smart. One of the most debilitating assumptions that we make is that we are "normal" and that others are not. Our hypothesis is that the world should look to our employees as it looks to us. We believe they want to be treated the way we want to be treated.

Stop it!

Do not treat them the way you want to be treated. Treat them as *they* want to be treated. Because there are three "negotiator" personality types within the Black Swan Method, two out of three employees or coworkers you deal with see *themselves* as the "normal" one, not you. This means there is a minimum 66 percent chance the person you engage within a difficult conversation has an approach to conflict vastly different from yours.

When we think "I am normal," we unconsciously project our own ideals and sensibilities on other people, including our employees.

For example, you say to yourself that because you like pepperoni pizza, others should also like pepperoni pizza. It only makes sense, right? Pepperoni is delicious!

Wrong!

What is "normal" is unique to the individual.

Recognizing which type you are and the type you are dealing with will help you appreciate their definition of "normal."

At the BSG, we have conducted an exercise for businesspeople all over the globe. The exercise involves exposing them to our three negotiator personality types. Then, upon introspection, they place themselves into one of the categories. Without fail we have found that each group splits fairly neatly into thirds.

The first type is strongly predisposed to being heard and respected and competing to win at all costs. They have an aggressive communication style and low regard for future relationships.

The second type gets tremendous satisfaction from relationships. Having others like them is more important than accomplishments.

The third type is a reserved problem-solver, more concerned with data and information. They do not slink away from conflict, but they consider it largely a waste of time. Tell them what the issue is, and they would much prefer to fly solo in coming up with a solution.

Let's take a look at each more closely.

IDENTIFYING THEIR TYPE

How do you identify each type? When you have skin in the game, the pressure is on, or you feel you are getting backed into a corner or attacked, what is your default type? As I lay out the characteristics of each, consider which best fits your human-nature response.

Here is a story that may help you decide which one you are.

Imagine your conflict is a giant grizzly bear. You are hiking in the woods and come across this bear. He is sitting on the path you are walking on. You see him. He sees you. The *Assertive* unsheathes a large hunting knife and says to herself, "I may not win this one, but at the end, this bear is going to know he has been in a fight."

The *Analyst* pulls out his GPS unit and begins to scroll through the different escape paths off the main one that he entered prior to the hike for an emergency like this. He ducks behind a tree, selects a path, and moves deeper into the bush. He finds a tree to climb, removes a rifle from his pack, and shoots the bear from a distance.

The *Accommodator* approaches the bear with arms extended and says, "There, there, little fella. You know what your problem is? No one understood you as a cub. I am gonna take you home, clean you up, and introduce you to my family." Understanding your negotiator conflict management personality is critical to navigating difficult conversations.

I am not suggesting you should or can change your personality. You are who you are. Your response to push back, attack, or flee is a part of your makeup.

The goal is not to change you. The goal is to make you aware of who you are and what the other two look like so you can borrow from the other two camps and make yourself better at interpersonal communications.

Recognize what style the other party adopts and how you should respond.

Understand that your strengths could be your greatest weakness.

TAKEAWAYS

- Tactical Empathy begins with the AA and attacking the negative emotion, impression, assumption, or opinion.

- The AA will demonstrate that you are trying to view things from the other person's frame of reference.

- Our attitudes, decision-making, and behavior are heavily influenced by negatives.

- Difficult conversation outline:

- Go all in. Have ten AAs, and use all ten.

- If you choose to leave some off of the list, those are the ones that will be a distraction.

- Summarize the relationship.

- AA: Get out in front of the negatives.

- Why? Ask a why question, if applicable, to get them to support your position.

- AA: Hit them with one or two more right before you get to your ask idea or change.

- Case in chief: Make your ask or state your objective.

- Types:

  - Assertives want to be heard and respected. Future relationships are unimportant.

  - Accommodators want to like and be liked. Maintaining relationships is their focus.

  - Analysts want to confirm facts and information as well as gather more. Relationships are just another factor to consider.

ACCUSATIONS AUDIT TABLE

	Assertives	Accommodators	Analysts
1	Many of you will find yourselves in this category. Several have been highlighted in this book. What is as important for the Assertive as resolving the issue? **Being heard and respected.**	What is as important for the Accommodator as resolving the issue? **Likability and maintaining relationships.** If there is no resolution of the issues discussed, they are okay with it as long as they leave on good terms.	What is as important for the Analyst as resolving the issue? **Confirming the facts and information** they already have.
2	Think of themselves as among the smartest people in the room.	Cannot move forward unless the relationship is good.	Readily conceal information.
3	View themselves as logical, straightforward, and goal-oriented. They say, "I want to talk to you so you can understand my logic."	Get satisfaction from solving others' problems.	Suspicious of motivations behind questions if there is no preexisting relationship. They ask themselves, *Why did you ask me that?*
4	The most inflexible.	The most aware of equity. Take a hard look at the other side's perspective of to make sure they are treating them fairly.	Like to agree in principle, but that does not mean the issue is resolved. They have agreed to think about it. Their yes is usually a maybe.

	Assertives	Accommodators	Analysts
5	Tunnel vision when trying to reach goals, which usually leads to missed opportunities. Have decided where they want to end up. There is no range of options.	When you are being a jerk, Accommodators will not tell you because they do not want to offend you. Tell you you are right even when they are not buying into what you are saying for the same reason.	Do not like to be pushed or led, so how do you get them to open up? Engage them in comparative analysis. They love to explain the rationale for how they got to where they are.
6	No cost is too high for the win. Do not leave the room until a resolution has been reached.	Good use of time is conversation. If they are in a friendly conversation and building or maintaining a relationship, they are being productive.	Take as much as is necessary to get it right. While Assertives want a yes and do not care about the how, Analysts do not work like that. They want the how. Time is also an opportunity to think. When thinking, they fall silent.
7	Do not display empathy but are highly vulnerable to it.	More attuned to kinesics and verbal signals.	High tolerance for assertive, hard-nosed discussions. They tend to overprepare, lining up facts, data, and information.

	Assertives	Accommodators	Analysts
8	Not the same as aggressive, but because they have a direct style of communication that they employ aggressively, people equate assertion with aggression. To Assertives, directness provides less opportunity for miscommunication.	Hypersensitive to how they deliver their message. The last thing they want to do is to say something negative that could upset another person. If pushed on something or asked to agree to something where they have no authority, body language shows their hesitancy (nothing verbal).	Do not fear interpersonal conflict or heated discussion of objectives, but they do view it as a waste of time.
9	Will not stab you in the back. Prefer to walk up and bury the knife in your chest so they can see the look in your eyes.	Beholden to the white lie. One Accommodator told us, "We are not intentionally lying to you, but you cannot believe everything that we say." They want to make you happy, so they agree to everything. They even overpromise and agree to something they cannot implement because in the moment they want to appease you or they want to be fair.	
10	When a conversation goes bad or is unproductive and you ask them what went wrong, they say they were not assertive enough.	When a conversation goes bad or is unproductive and you ask them what went wrong, they say they did not focus enough on the relationship.	When a conversation goes bad or is unproductive and you ask them what went wrong, they say they either did not have enough information or the other side failed to see the logic.

	Assertives	Accommodators	Analysts
11	Do not appreciate the currency of an apology. It implies they did something wrong.	They appreciate the currency of an apology, both in giving and receiving.	
12	Assertives and Analysts are two sides of the same coin. Therefore, Assertives hate dealing with Analysts and vice versa. Love dealing with Accommodators because Accommodators are so focused on the relationship that they will get beaten up for a while, which is right up the Assertives' alley.	Enjoys working with the two other types, to a point.	Both Analysts and Assertives view themselves as logical. The problem is logic is often based on your frame of reference. If you think you are logical, and I think I am logical, yet we do not agree, somebody's facts are wrong. Instead of logical, pragmatic is a better descriptor for the Analysts.

	Assertives	Accommodators	Analysts
13	Because they love to talk, the technique of Silence has less of an effect on them because you shutting up means you want them to continue talking.	Silence makes them nervous. When they are met with it, they immediately ask themselves what went wrong. *What is the problem? What did I do? Did I offend them? Maybe I need to apologize.*	Should make their use of Silence a part of their AA. When talking to an Assertive, the Analyst should say something like, "This is going to sound stupid. I tend to fall silent during conversations. It is not that I necessarily want you to continue talking. I do it to further process what was just said." When talking to an Accommodator, the Analyst should say something like, "This is going to sound horrible. I tend to fall silent during conversations. It does not mean that you have upset me or made me angry. I do it to further process what was just said." Note the deliberate use of the words "stupid" for the Assertive and "horrible" for the Accommodator. They are likely the adjectives that each thinks of often.

	Assertives	Accommodators	Analysts
14	When it comes to reciprocity, once you give in to the Assertive, they are not satisfied. They count the seconds until you give them something else. "I got a piece, and I want more."	The most reciprocal of the three types.	Least reciprocal of the three in large part because they think of reciprocity as a trap. If you make a concession for an Analyst that they were not prepared for or did not factor into their thinking in some way, their first thought is, *Something has got to be wrong with this.* On the other hand, they do not give anything up unless they have thought about it long and hard. They do not give it up because it means something to you. They do not give up because you have laid out unbeatable logic. They offer concessions only when it makes sense to them.
15	Take nothing personal during a heated discussion. They will argue vehemently and then go for a beer with the other person afterward.	Can be vicious in certain situations. Once they recognize there is no relationship to be developed or their tolerance level for being burned has been reached, they can be very aggressive.	Autonomous. If they can do it by themselves, they will.

	Assertives	**Accommodators**	**Analysts**
16	Coming to a resolution or gaining compliance is more important than future relationships. Respect is more important than resolution or compliance.	Maintaining the relationship is more important than compliance or resolution.	View relationships as something to be managed but not the most important thing.
17	Attorneys, investment bankers, venture capitalists, surgeons, and car salespeople are where you can find Assertives.	Social workers, teachers, and counselors are where you can find Accommodators.	IT professionals, entrepreneurs, and engineers are where you can find Analysts.
18	The best tools for having difficult conversations with Assertives: Mirrors help them to connect their thoughts. They come in talking to make you understand. Use Mirrors to help them get their thoughts out for clarity. Mirrors also feed their egos since the words you Mirror are their own. They love the way they sound. CQs: What and how questions feed their need to talk. Summarize: Let them know you are picking up what they are laying down. Try to get a "that is right" out of them.	The best tools for having difficult conversations with Accommodators: CQs: Use what and how questions to focus on implementation. Maybe they have not been as candid because they do not want to upset the relationship. What and how questions give them permission to open up.	The best tools for having difficult conversations with Analysts: Labels: Use Labels that focus on comparative analysis. "It seems like you have put a lot of effort into coming up with an alternative solution." "It looks like you have a really good handle on this." It is not confrontational, and you recognize their problem-solving ability and their ability to focus on the facts.

CHAPTER 13

THE BEST OF THE REST

THERE ARE SOME ADDITIONAL SKILLS YOU SHOULD ADOPT to help you better navigate tough conversations. Outlined in this chapter are techniques to address counterproductive behavior, saying no, gauging the yes, and summarizing.

I-MESSAGES

I-Messages are used to confront counterproductive behavior without being confrontational. They express to the other person how it makes you feel when they do or say certain things.

These can be effective responses to the other person when they are in attack mode, and at some point in any difficult conversation, you will get attacked. Count on it. By simply saying, "When you [the objectionable behavior], I feel [whatever you are feeling] because [the effect it is having]."

Consider the following fictitious scenarios.

Rachel's IT team worked for months researching three software options their company might use to handle HR complaints and investigations. They analyzed the costs and benefits for each one and strongly recommended the software that was the most expensive initially but would yield the most benefit in the long term as the company grew.

When the C-suite reviewed the recommendation, they opted to go with the cheapest one. They said that investing in the recommended solution would result in a short-term fiscal risk. Rachel did not agree, but she understood. Because her team had put in considerable time and deliberation before making the recommendation, she wanted an opportunity to explain the team's rationale to her boss. She is an Analyst.

A meeting was set, and Rachel arrived with all the data to support her position. Each time her boss tried to ask a question, Rachel cut him off. As the conversation progressed, Rachel became more animated.

Productive discourse was not happening. As Rachel took a deep breath, her boss seized the moment. "Rachel," he said, "when you keep interrupting me, I get frustrated because it seems like you are not here to talk with me but at me."

Rachel sat silently for a few seconds and then offered an apology.

Placing the "when you" before the "I feel" is a departure from other examples of I-Messages. I believe that verbal syntax is important. Therefore, saying "when you" at the beginning of the statement provides a subtle reminder that we are still operating from the other person's frame of reference. It maintains an atmosphere of respect because it demonstrates that our reaction was based on something they produced.

Experience has shown more positive responses if the "when you" is placed at the front of the statement as opposed to the "I feel."

I-Messages allow us to address persistent or uncooperative behavior in a nonthreatening fashion, which, in turn, maintains our ability to influence. With the I-Message, you are telling them to knock it off without telling them to knock it off.

When you are engaged in a difficult conversation, chances are that the other side will try to bait you into an argument. Persistent counterproductive behavior damages your credibility as a leader the longer it goes unaddressed. Avoid being pulled into an argument or trading personal attacks with them. An argumentative, sarcastic, or hostile tone will reinforce the negatives harbored by the other side and cause them to rationalize their behavior.

Brittany was conducting a presentation for her boss and ten colleagues when, midsentence, a coworker interrupted her to say he did not think her proposal would work. She told him she would open the discussion up for questions at the conclusion of the presentation.

A few minutes later, the same coworker stood up and walked toward the front of the room, stating why he thought she was off base. Brittany fired back, "When you interrupt me like that, I get distracted because it derails my train of thought." She followed it with a no-oriented question: "Would it be horrible if you saved your comments until the end and allowed me to continue with what I am saying first?"

The offending coworker sulked back to his seat and never said another word.

The I-Message personalizes you, moving you beyond a leader trying to impose your will, to just being a person.

NO-ORIENTED QUESTIONS

Yes is commitment, and no is protection. When asking a verb-led question, you are pushing for a yes. This puts a sense of obligation on the other person. Their autonomy is being encroached upon, which can understandably lead to resentment.

No instantly makes people feel safe, while yes makes them worry about they have committed themselves. Nearly every yes is a conditional yes at best and a counterfeit yes at worst.

No is always no, so why not make that work for you to break an impasse, get someone's attention, or help someone think clearly?

Just change your yes-oriented-question ("Can I use your car?") to a no-oriented question ("Would it be a bad idea if I used your car?")

Pushing for a yes via verb-led questions is self-defeating behavior. Most of your yes-oriented questions can simply be flipped to get the same result you want by changing the beginning of them to:

- "Is it ridiculous...?"

- "Would it be horrible...?"

- "Is it a bad idea...?"

- "Have you given up on...?"

Using no-oriented questions is yet another demonstration that you are trying to see the world through the other person's eyes.

Imagine the conversation in which you must tell your top performer she is only going to get a 3 percent raise as opposed to an anticipated 5 percent increase based on new budget parameters for increases.

"Sam, this is going to sound terrible (AA). I am limited in what I can give you in terms of cash compensation. I am committed to rewarding you for your outstanding performance. Would it be ridiculous if I shared with you some of the ideas I have to show our appreciation for your accomplishments?"

Or "Sam, I am committed to helping you achieve the professional goals you have for your career. Is it a bad idea if we talked about where you would like to be in the next couple of years in your career and how I can help you get there?"

PHASES OF NO

Even the nicest leaders in the world will still have to say no to their employees from time to time. You will reject employees for a myriad of reasons. If there are staffing issues, you will deny leave requests. If there are budget constraints, you will turn down requests for training or travel. Yes, you want to encourage collaboration and brainstorming, but sometimes decisions have already been made and it is time to execute.

It does not mean you are a jerk. It means you are doing what is right for the organization. However, hearing no from the boss can be demoralizing, especially when employees believe that you owe them a yes. Tell your hardworking direct report who has logged twenty hours of overtime this month that she cannot take that much-deserved family vacation, and you are basically telling her to disengage. Do it enough times, and she is off to work for someone else.

Nobody who is successful in any profession can avoid these types of scenarios. Not saying no when you have to causes the person with whom you are dealing to proceed with false assumptions. These will be viewed as traps or even betrayals that will be resented when exposed.

How you turn employees down can make a huge difference in how they react. It is important to remember that how you leave them after your current interaction can have an important influence on your next interaction. The last impression is the lasting impression.

They will not remember as much about the conversation as they will how it made them *feel*. Leaving your employee with a feeling of having been heard and treated with respect enhances your reputation as a leader. Setting boundaries, confronting, and saying no in a well-designed and even graceful manner changes the way people view you.

Here is an example from a Hollywood movie:

Bad guy: What do I want? Let's see. How about, can I see a priest?

Good guy: No, you cannot see a priest.

Bad guy: That is good, [Good guy]. You should not let me see a priest. A priest is associated with death and you do not want me thinking about death. But you told me no, [Good guy]. You cannot say no. Never use no in a hostage situation.

Good guy: Danny, would you relax a little bit?

Bad guy: I am relaxed! But here is some advice. Never say no to a hostage-taker. It is in the manual. Will you tell me no again?

Good guy: No.

Bad guy: Wrong answer! Never use no, do not, will not, or cannot. All right? It eliminates options. The option that leaves is to shoot someone. Understand?

Good guy: Yes.

Bad guy: Yes! Good! See, yes is good. You say no again, I will kill somebody. Let's practice. Can I see a priest?

Good guy: You know what? Can we just talk about this right now?

Bad guy: You wanted to talk! We are talking! Now, can I see a priest?

Good guy: I will see what I can do.

Bad guy: That is good, [Good guy]. Now you are learning. I would like a submachine gun to blow everyone away.

Good guy: I will look into that.

Bad guy: You are doing good. You ever cheat on your wife?

Good guy: No.

Bad guy: Watch yourself. I will kill someone. You ever cheat on your wife? Answer!

Good guy: I will see what I can do. I will have to think about that. I will look into that.

The only thing that makes this back-and-forth bearable is, of course, it is fictitious. Just like in the good guy's case, in the real world we refrain from telling a hostage-taker no outright because we have devised ways to say it without saying it. Expressing it in a manner that invited collaboration and did not reject the hostage-taker personally.

Here is how you can say no as gently and as elegantly as possible without killing morale.

Phase 1: "How am I supposed to do that?"

This conveys no without cornering yourself or them. Tone of voice is critical because this phrase can be delivered as both an accusation or as a request for assistance.

The emphasis can be placed on the "how," "I," or "that" for very different effects. Depending on the circumstances, you may find it necessary to ask this question several times, with emphasis being placed on different words each time.

This also tends to have the effect of making the other side take a good look at your situation. We call this "forced empathy." They will be less resistant to the no because of it. Forced empathy is the reciprocal empathy they show because you have consistently demonstrated Tactical Empathy. You are reaping the benefits of investing in it first.

Phase 2: "I am sorry. That just does not work for me."

This is another manner of saying no. It is a little more direct, retains the apology as a means of taking the edge off of the message, and keeps the focus on the situation.

Phase 3: "It sounds like you are in a tough spot. I am sorry. I am afraid I just cannot do that."

Notice Tactical Empathy on the front end. "It sounds like you are in a tough spot. I am sorry. I am afraid..." and assertiveness bringing up the rear with, "I just cannot do that."

Labeling your employee's circumstances on the front end of an assertive no statement continues the Tactical Empathy because their innate desire to have another understand is alive and well.

Here, "I am sorry" is important. Ego and authority may tell you apologies are signs of weakness. They imply that you made a mistake. Ego and authority hate that. The reality is that apologies are neutral. The issue is when, how, and why they are used.

When linked to assertion or confrontation, they are effective at softening the blow.

The "I" portion of this statement is designed to bring the focus back to you. It does a great job of removing their justifications as reasons you should say yes. Keeping the focus on your situation tends to limit arguments from the employee and invites them to see things from your point of view.

Phase 4: "I am sorry. No."

This is a slightly more succinct version of the above. If delivered gently, this is completely acceptable.

Phase 5: "No."

The last, most direct way of saying it is just to say it. It is not meant to be, "No!" Verbally, it should be delivered with a downward inflection and regard.

PARAPHRASING PLUS LABELING

If you can summarize your employees' circumstances so well that they respond with "That is right," "Absolutely," or "Hell yeah!" you are in a good spot. A good summary will receive a definitive confirmation. Hearing "You are right" is not as effective. If you can grasp this distinction, you are that much smarter during difficult conversations.

A summary is a combination of Labeling and Paraphrasing. It is summarizing what you have heard so far or know to be the case (Paraphrasing) and how the other person feels about the situation (Labeling).

This indicates two important things. You are listening to them accurately, and maybe even more importantly, they realize you are listening. It also shows you have a good grasp on the circumstances, and it provides them an opportunity to fill in anything you may have missed.

On an unconscious level, they genuinely appreciate it.

Here is what is wrong with "you are right" and why we are often seduced by it. First, we all *love* being right. It can be as intoxicating as getting a yes and often gives a feeling of great accomplishment. In many cases, we *are* right! So why not be given credit for it?

The truth is that when someone says "You are right" to the boss it is because, well, you are the boss. They defer to your position of authority over them. Another reason is that as the boss, you have probably been taking an argument-based approach, and you are pushing your point on them. You are showing them you are smarter than they are.

Unfortunately, human nature being what it is, this does not bode well for compliance, agreement, or buy-in as your employees will be much more interested in their ideas than they will yours. Think of the number of times you have said "You are right" to someone else just to get them to shut up and leave you alone.

They have been unrelenting in their approach. The only way you could get them to end it was to issue a "You are right." They then got a happy look on their face and went away, and you went back to what you were doing.

How many times have you worked very hard to get an employee to see the reason and logic of your thinking and had them respond with "You are right," only to find they did not change any of the behavior you had been trying to get them to change?

Put this into action and find out for yourself. Fully summarize the employee's position, both in content (Paraphrasing) and how they feel about it (Labeling) until the only possible response they have is a definitive confirmation like, "That is right." You will remove false obstacles and create turning points in your relationship that benefit your objectives.

THE RULE OF THREE

If yes is a success, what is no? We often ask people we are training this question. The most common response is that no is a failure.

Some people believe the word "yes" is one of the most beautiful words in the English language. It is the word we most often desire because we think it means we got our way.

The desire to hear it blinds us to what is really being said. When implementing the change or otherwise looking for buy-in, leaders often frame it in a "yes-able" proposition. This is widely misinterpreted into the ridiculous idea of building yes momentum. It says that if you get people to say yes three times in a row, momentum has built to the point that when you ask them to buy in, they will automatically say yes!

It is so prevalent in argument construction that the moment anyone starts to try to get us to say yes, our guard goes up.

Most CEQs we hear or use are designed in this fashion. The questioner is quite clearly pushing for a yes. While this may be a good strategy for interrogating a suspect during an investigation, it is not a good strategy for difficult or significant conversations. It diminishes rapport and impedes the building of trust-based influence.

Think about the last time you were on the receiving end of this verb-led question. You are in your office and the phone rings. You answer, and the person says, "Hey, Eric, have you got a minute to talk?" Three things go through your mind almost immediately.

First, you wonder, *How long is a minute?*

Second, you wonder, *If I have a minute to talk, do I want to talk to you?*

Third, you wonder, *If I want to talk to you, do I want to talk about what you want to talk about?*

Clearly it is a good time for the caller to talk or else she would not have called. Eric knows saying yes will obligate him, in the short term. No one likes the feeling of forced obligation.

Have you ever heard a yes and found out later it was not a yes but a no in waiting? There are three kinds of yeses:

- Counterfeit

- Confirmation

- Commitment

Since people are so used to others trying to drive them into commitment yeses, they liberally dole out counterfeit yeses like they were Tic-Tacs. The counterfeit yes is often used because the other person wants to gather more information from you before they tell you no. Many of your employees will acquiesce and give you a counterfeit yes just to keep you happy. Remember: the first yes you are given by anyone, employee or otherwise, should be considered counterfeit. It should be tested.

The first time you get a yes—for example, when an employee tells you they will have something for you by next Tuesday—try to Mirror it: "Next Tuesday?" Or Label it: "It seems like next Tuesday is good for you." They may respond with a yes: "Tuesday is my first day back. I will meet with the team then, and we will come up with a game plan." This is your second yes: the commitment.

To get to your third yes, Paraphrase: "So if I understand you correctly, Tuesday will be your first opportunity to discuss with the team what we agreed upon, and sometime Tuesday evening I will have something in my inbox from you." If they responded to this with a yes, this is your confirmation yes. Your agreement is more likely to be held up.

The Rule of Three provides proof of life of the agreement.

OBSTACLES TO AGREEMENT

Unsatisfied needs are emotional. You cannot direct your employees' decision-making until you deal with the emotional aspects of the circumstances as they see it.

Fear of losing face: Your direct reports will look to you to provide them with some dignity during and after a significant conversation.

Feeling misunderstood, maligned, mistreated, or aggrieved: At times you will encounter the toxic employee who feels that the difficult conversation is a result of you, the organization, or some other person being out to get them. Whether it is real or perceived does not matter because it is their frame of reference.

Everything you say and do should be considered based on its impact upon your people or peers. Their perceptions count. Not yours!

Whatever they view as a threat, confusing, or unfair is just that.

OTHER HNL STRATEGIES

- Be supportive.

- If you are not sure what someone meant, ask a Calibrated Question.

- Avoid saying no until absolutely necessary. Lower expectations. "I will take that under consideration, but it may be a problem."

- Avoid the distraction of your inner monologue.

- Be honest.

- Be humble.

- Repeat what they are looking for, but soften or reframe it.

- Do not raise aspirations or expectations.

- Be prepared to suggest alternatives.

TAKEAWAYS

- I-Messages are used to confront without being confrontational. They allow you to address uncooperative behavior without pointing a finger.

- Yes is commitment, and no is protection. No instantly makes people feel safe, while yes makes them worry about the commitment they have made. Use no to your advantage by asking no-oriented questions to trigger the safety of no.

- Setting boundaries, confronting, and saying no in a well-designed manner conveys a no without cornering you or them.

- Use Paraphrasing and Labels to summarize their feelings and circumstances so well that the only way they can respond is with, "That is right!"

- There are three types of yeses: counterfeit, commitment, and confirmation. Use the Rule of Three to determine which one you have been given. Label, Mirror, and Paraphrase each one to determine the viability of your agreement.

CHAPTER 14

THE HOSTAGE NEGOTIATOR LEADER

CONCLUSION

"Most of the successful people I've known are the ones who do more listening than talking."

—BERNARD MANNES BARUCH

I WROTE *EGO, AUTHORITY, FAILURE* TO SHOW THAT SUBORDINATING yourself to your employees, keeping your ego and authority in check, and practicing Tactical Empathy are the most efficient and sustainable ways to increase your leadership performance. Using the skills mentioned in the final chapters, you will create a working environment that engages, respects, and motivates your team members.

The fact that you picked up this book shows a desire to increase your EQ and equip yourself with interpersonal skills to demonstrate Tactical Empathy. If you go out and apply these practices today, you will be performing at a level higher than the majority of the leaders out there. If all you remember after reading this is that it is not about you when you engage in a significant conversation, you will increase your chances of positively influencing those under your charge.

Your EQ and Tactical Empathy should also increase because you have been exposed to several examples of abhorrent leader behavior. You likely recognized their similarity to those you work with or for. Perhaps it is you. If so, through those stories, you have been reminded of what not to do or what you need to change.

Repetition is the key to continual improvement. The skills in the last four chapters may feel awkward when you begin to use them. But stay with it; practicing develops the pathways. The skills do not take a lot of time to practice. I tell all new coaching clients to practice them in conversations that do not mean anything, where nothing is at stake or hanging in the balance—at the coffee shop, picking up dry cleaning, getting the car serviced, or whatever.

In those environments you are free to practice these skills without risk. Once you use one and it produces the desired effect, it is just like seeing a unicorn for the first time. You will not be able to wait until you can do it again. The more success you achieve, the more you will want to employ these skills. Then you will be ready to address your employees from a different frame of reference that will surprise and please them.

If you are new to the sport and you go to a basketball court to shoot free throws, your first dozen will be less than successful. But as you approach five or six dozen, your proficiency will increase.

If you do that for three weeks straight, it will be off the charts. The same is true with the hostage negotiation skills highlighted in this book. After sixty-seven repetitions, you will feel different, and others will begin to notice.

Use the skills with strangers and family members. Sit back and listen to them comment about something being strikingly different about you.

As you embark on this new brand of divergent leadership, remember that ego and authority are like the Force in *Star Wars*. They can be used for good or evil. Those who underestimate their intoxicating powers will never reach their full potential. Your ego and authority should be treated as living, breathing things. Each is committed to its own survival. They do not like to lose power over you. They will try to convince you that if you do not wield them like a broadsword, you will fail. They will also tell you that to achieve the brass ring at the next level, you have to view the world through your own prism at the expense of all others. It is my hope that you will no longer make yourself vulnerable to their seductions.

Ego and authority will never go away. Nor should they. They are a part of your makeup and at least deserve some credit for your success. Now that you have read this, I hope you have a better understanding of both so that they do not dominate your consciousness as much as they do toxic leaders.

Do not feel discouraged if ego and authority rear their heads from time to time. In some instances, when time is of the essence and the stakes are high, ego and authority are necessary. When the circumstances dictate that immediate, decisive action is required, your ego and authority should be front and center.

THE NEW YOU: THE HOSTAGE NEGOTIATOR LEADER

By taking stock of the cautionary tales of toxic leadership and practicing the skills, I trust you will become a deeper listener and take the time to understand the perspective of the person with whom you are dealing. Your transformation into Hostage Negotiator Leader will not be easy. In fourteen short chapters, I have tried to change the way you think about communicating with your direct reports after years if not decades of doing things your way. That is a lot of "doing" to undo.

The Hostage Negotiator Leader comprehends the necessity of putting their goals and objectives on the back burner to subordinate themselves to their employees in the context of a difficult conversation. Building strong superior–subordinate relationships, gathering information, and promoting morale takes time. It takes commitment, courage, and a lot of trust.

Few leadership attributes are more important than demonstrating Tactical Empathy—establishing rapport, building trust-based influence, and maintaining relationships with your direct reports. The Hostage Negotiator Leader gets that meaningful relationship, and influence starts with respect.

As a Hostage Negotiator Leader, you realize that in order to subordinate yourself to your employees, it cannot be about you. Your ego and authority will keep the embers of ambition and confidence glowing. But as a Hostage Negotiator Leader, you will not provide oxygen to reignite the flames unless it is in the best interest of your team and your organization.

You are now focused on channeling your self-confidence into working on behalf of those you are privileged to lead. The Hostage Negotiator Leader embraces humility. Humility encourages trust. With trust, almost anything is possible.

Humility means staying late to show an employee how to do something. It means taking overwhelming pressures from them.

You are now more attuned to inclusion. Inclusion produces more informed decisions and promotes creativity on the part of team members. Inclusive leadership encourages and enables individuals and groups to contribute to their fullest potential. It also encourages the capitalization of unique experiences, perspectives, and viewpoints for the benefit of the team and the organization.

Demonstrating true humility and EQ will help people see that you are inclusive. You are inviting everyone to be a part of the success of the organization rather than just "do what they are told." Negative command and control impede creativity and adversely affect morale.

The Hostage Negotiator Leader will lead by listening and asking CQs to challenge and change the conversation. This creates a culture where the organization interacts with one another human to human rather than title to title or rank to rank.

The Hostage Negotiator Leader is self-aware. You appreciate your strengths, weaknesses, and triggers. You keep your emotions in check, and most importantly, you know the impact your words, behavior, and emotions have on others. You welcome feedback. You are aware of how you are perceived. You know your blind spots.

You are hypersensitive to reading people and situations accurately. You understand your people and know how to get the best out of them. You can connect with your team by forgiving past mistakes, putting previous bad blood behind you, getting over petty resentments, and cheerleading when cheerleading is in order.

When everything goes right, you give away all the credit, and when everything goes wrong, you take all the responsibility. Instead of blowing your stack and taking over, the Hostage Negotiator Leader says, "Try again."

The Hostage Negotiator Leader knows that they are not responsible for the job. They are responsible for the people who do the job. They are examples of the types of leaders who will be emulated by those who follow them and will one day become leaders.

I hope they will become the kind of leaders who are so self-aware, humble, emotionally intelligent, and inclusive that this book will become obsolete.

ACKNOWLEDGMENTS

I WOULD LIKE TO EXPRESS MY GRATITUDE TO THE MANY PEOPLE who saw me through this process—to all those who provided support, talked things over, read, wrote, offered comments, allowed me to quote their remarks, and assisted in the editing, proofreading, and design.

First and foremost, thank you to my beautiful wife, Nichole, for standing beside me throughout my career. You supported and encouraged me in spite of the frequency with which it took me away from you and the girls at the least convenient times. You put everything on hold for me while I played cop and never batted an eye, even though I gave you every reason to. Your patience with me never wavered as I transitioned into this latest endeavor. What you have done and who you are to me I could never adequately express.

My loving daughters, Morgan and Taylor. *Quia amor, auxilium, et solatium habeamus constant.* You have always been my biggest cheerleaders, making me feel bigger and better than I am. I am so proud of the ladies you have become.

To my wonderful mom, Linda: without your support, this would not have happened. As a single mother, you probably never would have imagined that your knuckle-headed son would become an author. Because of what you taught me and what you espoused as I grew, look at me now!

Special thanks to Chris Voss, my mentor, my friend, my boss. You saw something in me that few others have over the course of my career. Your confidence in my ability and potential was a direct contributor to this book. It would be impossible for me to count all the ways you have helped me in both my first and second careers. Consider me eternally grateful.

Professor Eric Koester, for inspiring me to publish this book. There were many times during the process when I questioned my worth, my writing, my (as it appeared at the time) waste of time. Through it all you continued to push and encourage. I have not been coached like that since high school. That and all the other ancillary things you and your staff did made this possible. Because of you I can legitimately hang the word "author" at the end of my name. How cool is that? Thank you.

Robyn Nichols. You and I both know you could have easily written this. You taught me more about what a leader should be than anyone else I have ever worked for, not because you preached it but because you modeled it. I have always said if I became just half the leader you are, I would be okay. Thank you for your belief in me when I was your boss. When you were mine. When we worked side by side. People often ask what I miss most about not being "on the job." It is working with you.

Marcela Oakley for nagging, nagging, nagging me to write this. As I think back on it, you probably gave me the final push. You are a true student of the game, a consummate professional, and a great friend.

I would be remiss if I did not give a tip of the cap to all of the exceptional negotiators who came before me. You cut the path and made it easier for guys like me.

Last but not least, all of you whom I have worked with, around, and for over the course of my time on this planet whose names I have failed to mention: you all had a hand in this. Thank you for teaching me.

BONUS MATERIAL

HOSTAGE NEGOTIATOR PARENTING

I would there were no age between 16 and three and 20, or that youth would sleep out the rest for there's nothing in between but getting wenches with child, wronging the ancientry, stealing, fighting...
—WILLIAM SHAKESPEARE, *THE WINTER'S TALE*

PARENTS OF ADOLESCENTS WITH SERIOUS BEHAVIORAL problems often feel like hostages. A hostage-taking teenager can ruin their own life and the lives of their parents and siblings. "Difficult" teens are often sent away to expensive "programs," some of which can run over $100,000.

For many youngsters, the long-term success of these programs is questionable. Impoverished or even middle-class homes cannot afford long-term interventions on this scale. At best they get some counseling or some mind-numbing medications. A few lucky ones end up in a sports program with a great coach as a mentor.

What if there was something else—an actual method of intervention that worked to free teenagers from taking themselves and their parents hostage?

The skills espoused by the Black Swan Group have been tested and proven effective in changing the behavior of difficult adolescents in clinical settings. They will prove likewise in the home before a clinical setting becomes necessary.

It begins with understanding what is going on "upstairs" in the brain.

THE ADOLESCENT BRAIN

The generally accepted belief used to be that the vast majority of brain development took place in the first few years of life. As recently as the late 1990s, we did not have the ability to look inside the human brain and track development. Between then and now, significant advancements in brain imaging technologies have rectified that. With magnetic resonance imaging (MRI) and functional magnetic resonance imaging (fMRI), neuroscientists can now look inside the brain and track changes in both structure and function. MRIs take pictures while fMRIs take videos of brain activity, giving us robust representations of how the brain develops. This insight has changed the way scientists think about such development by revealing that the majority of it does not end in early childhood. Instead, the brain continues to develop throughout adolescence and into adulthood.

Adolescence is the transition period between childhood and adulthood. This period of life starts with the biological, hormonal, and physical changes of puberty. It ends when the individual attains stability and independence. During this time, dramatic changes occur in the prefrontal cortex (PFC). This region of the brain is involved in decision-making, planning, and inhibiting inappropriate behavior. It is also involved in self-awareness and understanding social interactions with other people.

MRI studies looking at the development of the PFC have shown that it undergoes dramatic changes during adolescence. The volume of gray matter declines significantly because the brain eliminates unnecessary connections between synapses. The brain gives itself a tune-up.

Scientists have examined brain scans of both adolescents and adults who were tasked with thinking about other people's mental and emotional states. They found that part of the PFC was more active in adolescents than it was in adults. They also learned that the activity decreased with age. These examinations have been conducted numerous times in labs around the world, and they all show the same thing. The activity in the medial PFC decreases during adolescence; therefore, the ability to consider someone else's perspective is still developing.

When your teenager displays a reluctance or refusal to consider other perspectives, seems self-absorbed, takes risks, or is moody, it's because their brain is not ready.

This has implications on how you should navigate tough conversations with your children.

During adolescence, when independence becomes increasingly important, tough conversations are around every corner. When "I want" or "I need" is in your head or your child's head, you are in a tough conversation.

In every tough conversation, there are negative dynamics and emotions at play. These are exacerbated by the underdeveloped PFC. Even as an adult with a fully functioning PFC, when your negative emotions are high, your rational thinking is low. Negative emotions are responses to real or perceived threats that activate the amygdala, which impedes what is supposed to be going on in the PFC. When you are triggered, you are dumber than you otherwise would be. Imagine how much more impactful those negative emotions and dynamics are for an adolescent.

As parents, we are going to do or say things that cause them to push back. That is just the way it is. How you respond to that pushback is what matters most.

Many parents get so caught up in trying to quash the resistance that they fail to look at what is motivating it.

When kids push back, parents often jump into explanation mode. When you are explaining, you are losing. The dissension will not go away unless you have addressed the negatives that are fueling it.

Be aggressive in your pursuit of understanding what is motivating your child's behavior. That understanding will enable you to navigate difficult conversations, improving your relationship along the way.

Communication is of the utmost importance in every relationship. This is especially true when it comes to your relationship with family, including adolescents. They are under tremendous pressures from peer or romantic relationships, future plans, or current performance issues, and other sources. They want you to understand what the lay of the land looks like from their perspective. How do you do it? Tactical Empathy.

TACTICAL EMPATHY:
THE SECRET TO HOSTAGE NEGOTIATOR-PARENTING

At its core, Hostage Negotiator-Parenting (HNP) is designed to change the way you think about communicating with your teen. It is you using Tactical Empathy and treating them with the same level of deference that hostage negotiators use with hostage-takers. It promotes a healthy home environment and, ultimately, achieves better outcomes.

Using the Black Swan Method, negative outcomes for and offensive behaviors by your teen can be managed or avoided altogether. Your ability to consciously and proactively identify your teen's perspective and articulate that recognition is key to improving or repairing your relationship.

Note the specific use of the words "articulate" and "recognition." Recognition of what the world looks like to them is the easy part. Articulation is where most parents falter. Intuitively they recognize what is going on with their child. Their "gut" tells them. According to Dr. Bruce Lipton, author of *Biology of Belief*, your conscious brain processes forty bits of information per second. Your gut (i.e., your subconscious brain) processes 20 million bits per second. It is you knowing without knowing how you know. Articulating your child's perspective ensures that they *know* you see them that way.

Maybe they made a bad choice and are dealing with the consequences or they did or said something that made you angry. Instead of solely looking at the behavior, stay curious, and try to find the motivation for the behavior or statement. If you stay genuinely curious during the conversation, it will be impossible for you to get triggered. Reaction is almost always emotional. Response is almost always rational. If you react negatively, it may discourage them from coming to you with similar issues in the future.

Avoid judgment, criticism, and lecturing. They often know they screwed up. Piling on, even if done out of love or concern, does not help. Label their circumstances or emotions before jumping to conclusions or making assumptions. Lecturing about how you handled similar situations when you were their age is a cheap attempt at common ground and can be counterproductive. Instead of bringing down Thor's hammer, just listen. Once you have done that, then you can work together toward the next steps.

Just because you should not lecture does not mean that you cannot offer support or advice.

In fact, that is your responsibility. It is just a matter of how you sequence the conversation. It is always Tactical Empathy first and support and advice second. You may simply state, "It seems like you have a vision for how you would like to see this play out." This is an "asking" Label used in place of, "What do you want to do now?" Teens are guarded by nature. They are suspicious of direct questions and often tell us only what they want us to know. You are more likely to get an unguarded answer when using a Label over a direct question.

The "asking" Label is followed by a No-Oriented Question, such as: "Are you against sharing that vision with me?" The word "vision" is used specifically in this instance because most of us are imaginative people, teens included. The word "vision" turns them into the narrator of the movie that is playing in their head. See how their response meshes with or diverges from the advice you are planning to give. Label, Mirror, or Paraphrase the portions of their response that line up with what you were thinking. The more it lines up, the less you have to say and the more buy-in you are likely to get because it will seem like their solution.

If it diverges, be careful not to offend. As an example, start with another No-Oriented Question, such as: "Are you against me walking you through what I was thinking?" After you receive the response, follow it with an Accusations Audit or three: "This is going to sound harsh. You are going to think I am way off base or trying to impose my will." Let that sit for a few seconds, and then provide them with your vision of how you think the issue should be resolved. Be ready to be attacked. In every difficult conversation, the chances of being attacked are real. Do not rise to the bait and attack back. Attacking back or other negative emotional reactions will fire up their already activated amygdala and further impede their ability to process. Likewise, you cannot flee—literally or figuratively. Moving off topic or disengaging means the negative dynamic has not been addressed and will return again. Stay in the moment, and figure out where it is coming from. An attack during a difficult conversation means they think you are not listening, you have not identified other pressures they are under, or they are trying to manipulate you. You have to figure out which one.

What if they refuse to open up?

Hit them with an Accusations Audit followed by a Label: "I know this is difficult for you. You probably think I will not understand. You seem incredibly guarded and probably think this is a waste of time." The silence is them telling you, *I do not trust you with this information,* for whatever reason. Again, focus on the motivation of the behavior, not the behavior itself. Ask yourself, *What are they telling me by not telling me?* If they are steadfast in their silence, do not push. Use a Label: "It seems like you are just not ready." Follow this statement with Dynamic Silence. Sometimes they need a little time and space to process emotions that are hard to convey at their age.

What if I am the cause of the current situation?

If you are (or you think you might be) the cause, apologize. Never underestimate the currency of an apology. Whether you believe you are at fault does not matter. If your kid believes you are at fault, then you are at fault. An apology will ratchet tension down in the home. It is the first step in returning your teen to their normal functioning level and showing them transparency and humility. That it is not about you.

Stay curious, and stay in control of yourself. The only aspect in any tough conversation that you have total control over is your emotions. Shut your mouth. Assume you have something to learn. Trust me: you do. We all hide information during tough conversations. Teens have mastered this. They are in possession of a multitude of Black Swans. The more you talk, the less you are learning. If it is a planned conversation, vent to someone else before engaging your teen. The more you get off your chest before you get into the room, the less will come out when you are in the room. Remember, your teen is not the problem. The issue is the problem.

Prepare to give them a hearing. By default, most adolescents think people (adults) do not understand them, and all of us want to be understood. Listening is the cheapest and most effective concession we can make for our kids with the endgame of showing respect. Focus on the process of navigating the conversation and understanding and satisfying their needs rather than "I am right. You are wrong."

Show them that you are not trying to walk in their shoes but rather see through their eyes. Try a Summary: "X, Y, and Z occurred, and as a result, you feel..." or "It sounds like that really made you upset." Being right is not the key; making the attempt to get it right is!

Adolescents are expressive by nature and are frequently hypervigilant, which is just a fancy way of saying they will be more apt to see through your BS. Your tone indicates your attitude and speaks louder than anything you may actually say. A calm, controlled demeanor is more effective than a brilliant argument.

Acknowledge their point and agree whenever you can, but remember agreement is not necessary. This will help to create a positive atmosphere for problem-solving.

Recognize your own culpability. How have you contributed to the current dynamic? What went wrong?

Begin the process of answering these questions with Accusations Audits and an apology. Something like, "I know I offended you. I am sorry," and "You think I am self-serving, rude, and condescending. You believe I do not appreciate what you are going through."

Next, invite them to talk using a No-Oriented Question. "Would it be ridiculous if we took a few minutes to clear the air?"

Follow this with a Summary, and then ask, "What am I missing?" Your kids love to point out when you are wrong. If you are missing anything, they will tell you. Listen carefully. If they take the time to correct you, they are sharing something that is important to them.

Next comes the "vision" Label to get to the catalyst of the conflict and what they think the next steps should be. You will Label, Mirror, or Paraphrase the response and follow with another No-Oriented Question, asking permission to share your vision.

Resolution: Is their agreement or buy-in on solid ground?

Once you have agreed on the resolution, use a Summary to cement the agreement. Follow that with a few Calibrated

Questions to test commitment to the agreement. "How will we know we are on track? What should we do if we are not?" Labeling and Mirroring the responses will solidify what was agreed upon.

Remember to be aware of common obstacles to agreement.

These can include:

- Unsatisfied emotional needs. We cannot direct a person's decision-making until we deal with the negative emotions as they see them. If you jump into problem-solving too soon, you will find yourself up against a kid who is not fully vested in the solution and not yet ready for agreement.

- Fear of losing face. Any resolution that even gives a hint of embarrassment will elicit resistance. They may be looking to you to provide them with some assurances that their dignity will be maintained.

- Feeling misunderstood or mistreated. Many adolescents feel this way, or they feel aggrieved or maligned. Whether real or perceived, it does not matter because you are operating from their frame of reference, not yours!

Tone

When you use Tactical Empathy in your day-to-day interactions with your kids, remember that how you say something is more important than what you say. Delivery plays a huge role in how it is received. Your kids need to hear sincerity and genuineness in your communications; otherwise your efforts will fall flat.

If you want to strengthen your relationship with your adolescent or you want to improve a relationship that has been damaged, there is no faster or easier way than using Tactical Empathy to demonstrate an understanding of their worldview and connect with them well enough to build trust-based influence.

BIBLIOGRAPHY

THE SOURCES BELOW ARE EITHER CITED IN THIS BOOK OR have strongly influenced its development.

Adubato, Steve. "Great Leaders Admit Their Mistakes." *Stand and Deliver.* https://www.stand-deliver.com/columns/team-building-mentoring-and-coaching/824-great-leaders-admit-their-mistakes.html (December 2018).

CareerCast.com, "The Least Stressful Jobs of 2018." https://www.careercast.com/jobs-rated/2018-least-stressful-jobs (November 2018).

Changingminds.org, "Genderlect" http://changingminds.org/explanations/gender/genderlect.htm (November 2018).

Coggins, E. "The History of Leadership Studies and Evolution of Leadership Theories." Tough Nickle. June 14, 2016. https://toughnickel.com/business/The-History-of-Leadership-Studies-and-Evolution-of-Leadership-Theories (August 2018).

Crisler, Jr., David. "Are You Trapped in Micromanagement?" *Law Enforcement Today*, October 10, 2013. https://www.lawenforcementtoday.com/are-you-trapped-in-micromanagement (August 2018).

Davenport, Mike. "Warning: Era Of The Abused Coach Needs To End." CoachingSporstToday.com, September 28, 2015. https://coachingsportstoday.com/warning-era-abused-coach-needs-end (December 2018).

Davis, Kelsie. "Bad Boss Index: The Worst Boss Behaviors, According to Employees [Infographic]." BambooHR. https://www.bamboohr.com/blog/bad-boss-index-the-worst-boss-behaviors-according-to-employees-infographic/ bamboohr.com (August 2018).

Dempsey, Martin. "'Heads Down, Thumbs Up' Is No Way To Go Through Life. We Need Our Leaders to Show Respect, Humility, and Inclusiveness," *Task and Purpose.* (February 2, 2018): https://taskandpurpose.com/we-need-our-leaders-to-show-respect-humility-and-inclusiveness.

Featherstone, Tony. "Ready to Lead? The Perils of Being Promoted Too Early." *The Sydney Morning Herald*, October 12, 2017. https://www.smh.com.au/business/workplace/perils-of-being-promoted-too-early-20171012-gyzils.html (August 2018).

Gentry, William, Weber, Todd and Sadri, Golnaz. "Empathy in the Workplace A Tool for Effective Leadership." *Center for Creative Leadership White Paper.* (November 2011) (https://www.ccl.org/wp-content/uploads/2015/04/EmpathyInTheWorkplace.pdf)

Headley, Jason. "It's Not about the Nail." Youtube. https://www.youtube.com/watch?v=-4EDhdAHrOg (July 2018).

Holt, Svetlana, Marques, Joan. "Empathy in Leadership: Appropriate or Misplaced? An Empirical Study on a Topic that Is Asking for Attention." *Journal of Business Ethics.* July 2012. https://www.researchgate.net/publication/225160079_Empathy_in_Leadership_Appropriate_or_Misplaced_An_Empirical_Study_on_a_Topic_That_is_Asking_for_Attention (July 2018).

Inskeep, Steve. "General. Martin Dempsey on Leadership and 'Radical Inclusion.'" Morning Edition. *National Public Radio,* March 8, 2008. https://www.npr.org/2018/03/08/591816699/gen-martin-dempsey-on-leadership-and-radical-inclusion (July 2018).

Lee, Bruce. "Be Like Water." Goodreads. https://www.goodreads.com/quotes/29138-be-like-water-making-its-way-through-cracks-do-not (June 2018).

Lipman, Victor. "How Important Is Empathy to Successful Management?" *Forbes*, February 24, 2018. https://www.forbes.com/sites/victorlipman/2018/02/24/how-important-is-empathy-to-successful-management/#40c1ba8ba46d (June 2018).

Neal, Steve. "Toxic Bully Boss: Straight Talk for Law Enforcement." *Law Officer*, February 16, 2016. http://lawofficer.com/leadership/toxic-bully-boss-straight-talk-for-law-enforcemen/ (July 2018).

NITV, Federal Services, "Why Rapport Building Is an Effective Strategy in Detainee Interviews." February 2017. https://www.cvsa1.com/interviewing-and-interrogation/why-rapport-building-is-an-effective-strategy-in-detainee-interview (June 2018).

McMains, Michael, Mullins, Wayman. "Crisis Negotiations: Managing Critical Incidents and Hostage Situations in Law Enforcement and Corrections, Fourth Edition." *Matthew Bender & Company, Inc., a member of the LexisNexis Group New Providence, NJ, 2010.* (November 2018).

Masters, Roy. "Harald Jahrling Back at Work with Rowing Australia." *Canberra Times*, June 18, 2016. https://www.canberratimes.com.au/sport/harald-jahrling-back-at-work-with-rowing-australia-20160617-gplj7v.html (July 2018).

Mayhew, Ruth. "The Importance of Feedback When in a Leadership Position." *Work - Chron.com*, http://work.chron.com/importance-feedback-leadership-position-3355.html. (November 2018).

O'Brien, John. "Dictator Who Insists On Trust and Togetherness." *Independent*, August 20, 2006. https://www.independent.ie/sport/dictator-who-insists-on-trust-and-togetherness-26415402.html (July 2018).

Picchi, Aimee. "9 Most Stressful American Jobs in 2018." *Money Watch,* CBS News, January 11, 2018. https://www.cbsnews.com/media/9-most-stressful-american-jobs-in-2018/ (September 2018).

Shmerling, Robert, MD. "Right Brain/Left Brain, Right?" *Harvard Medical School, Harvard Health Blog,* August 25, 2017. https://www.health.harvard.edu/blog/right-brainleft-brain-right-2017082512222 (December 2018).

Stutchbury, Greg. "I Pushed Myself Too Hard, Says 'Lay Down Sally.'" *Reuters*, May 1, 2008. https://www.reuters.com/article/us-olympics-australia-robbins/i-pushed-myself-too-hard-says-lay-down-sally-idUSSP34181920080501 (July 2018).

Watterson, Danny. "Why Emotional Intelligence Is The Best Indicator Of A Successful Hire." Vanderbloemen Search Group. https://www.vanderbloemen.com/blog/assessment-qualified-employees (June 2018).

Wilkins, Peter. "She's Not There." Australian Story. *Australian Broadcasting Company,* July 14, 2008. http://www.abc.net.au/austory/shes-not-there/9169070 (July 2018).

Wolfe, Alexander. "Is The Era Of Abusive College Coaches Finally Coming To An End?" *Sports Illustrated,* September 28, 2015. https://www.si.com/college-basketball/2015/09/29/end-abusive-coaches-college-football-basketball (August 2018).

Wong, Kristin. "Why It's So Hard to Admit You're Wrong." *New York Times,* May 22, 2017. https://www.nytimes.com/2017/05/22/smarter-living/why-its-so-hard-to-admit-youre-wrong.html. (November 2018).

Writer Unknown. "Former Coach Laments Errors In Robbins Affair" *The Sydney Morning Herald,* August 8, 2008. https://www.smh.com.au/sport/former-coach-laments-errors-in-robbins-affair-20080808-gdspm0.html (August 2018).